Fruitful

Fruitful

ESSENTIAL KEYS FOR THE MOST ABUNDANT CHRISTIAN LIFE

Jason J. Camacho

Xulon Press
2301 Lucien Way #415
Maitland, FL 32751
407.339.4217
www.xulonpress.com

© 2021 by Jason J. Camacho

All rights reserved solely by the author. The author guarantees all contents are original and do not infringe upon the legal rights of any other person or work. No part of this book may be reproduced in any form without the permission of the author. The views expressed in this book are not necessarily those of the publisher.

Due to the changing nature of the Internet, if there are any web addresses, links, or URLs included in this manuscript, these may have been altered and may no longer be accessible. The views and opinions shared in this book belong solely to the author and do not necessarily reflect those of the publisher. The publisher therefore disclaims responsibility for the views or opinions expressed within the work.

Unless otherwise noted, Scripture quotations are taken from The Holy Bible, English Standard Version, (ESV). Copyright © 2001 by Good News Publishers. Used by permission. All rights reserved.

In Scripture quotations, emphasis in bold was added by the author and was not part of the original translation.

Paperback ISBN-13: 978-1-6628-3723-4
Ebook ISBN-13: 978-1-6628-3724-1

Dedication:

To My Best Friend,

This book was only possible because of your hard work and dedication to being a faithful, God-honoring wife to me. I love you and God knows how thankful I am for you.

Table of Contents

Foundation: Where We're Going................... vii

Level 1: Purpose
Chapter 1: Be Fruitful 1
Chapter 2: Forbidden Fruit......................... 10
Chapter 3: Promised Seed 26
Chapter 4: Fruit Defined........................... 52

Level 2: Position
Chapter 5: New Identity 69
Chapter 6: Transformed Life....................... 87
Chapter 7: Heavenly Attributes 96

Level 3: Process
Chapter 8: Heart Posture.......................... 117
Chapter 9: Just Abide 135
Chapter 10: Controlled Fruit 150
Chapter 11: Divine Pruning 161
Chapter 12: Temptation Exposed 171
Chapter 13: The Fruitful Life..................... 193

Foundation:

Where We're Going

Something I've always wanted to do is create a practical resource that empowers new believers. This is why I developed this training and compiled it into one concise book. I want to give Christians the clearest, most helpful guide to living the fullest Christian life possible. This requires that believers understand what I believe to be some of the most essential teachings of the Christian faith. This includes the gospel message, our purpose in life, our position in Christ, and our process in time.

My goal is to teach you and empower you to live the best possible life this side of Heaven. This isn't about your best life now. This is about experiencing the fullest Christian life in preparation for eternity with God. God has more for you and I want you to walk in His abundant plan for your life.

I've come to realize that many issues for believers (and the church as a whole) result from the fact that they misunderstand key truths that are central to the Christian faith. We'll get to those key teachings in a moment. But first, I want you to know my heart behind this book.

The Origin Story

One of the most impactful series of sermons I've ever preached was titled "Abide" and it was communicated to my church's youth group. Most of the time I was preaching to myself, because those truths had yet to deeply penetrate my own heart. But, in spite of that reality, the overall consensus among our youth group was that this sermon series was the most enlightening and empowering set of biblical teachings that I had preached.

And, after processing this sermon series even deeper over the last few years, I realized that this collection of teachings was everything I've wanted in a complete resource for new believers. I had unknowingly developed a core faith training program for new believers.

Remember, I said that many issues for the Christian stem from a misunderstanding of essential Christian ideas. There are four ideas in particular that I believe have a tremendous impact on every individual's life, especially believers. These ideas are: the gospel message, our purpose, our position and our process. Let me briefly address the first issue.

Four Key Ideas

See, a misunderstanding of the basic gospel message can lead to many issues in a person's life. Think about it. Our view of God actually determines every single area of our life. Our view of God is like the thread that connects everything. How we live flows from how we view God. And, God is most clearly revealed in the person of The Son, Jesus Christ, (the second person of the trinity) through His death and resurrection.

Jesus and His saving work are the essential parts of the gospel message.

There is no good news of salvation without Jesus or His death, burial, and resurrection. Jesus is the gospel message of salvation. He is good news personified. So, if you misunderstand the foundation of your salvation and relationship with God, you'll end up spending much of your life confused, frustrated, and disappointed. Honestly, the gospel message becomes the lens through which you see this life.

Just as you'd look through a microscope or a telescope to see things as they actually are, so the gospel message of Jesus helps us to see our life and this world as they actually are. So, if you don't properly understand the gospel message, you'll see this life incorrectly because you're looking through a broken lens.

The second idea we have to unpack is this issue of our God-given purpose.

Every human being is created in the image of God for a divine purpose that God has determined. God, as the Creator, is the only one who has the right to decide the purpose of His creation. No one gets to decide the purpose of something except the creator (or inventor) of that thing.

We, as human beings are born into this world with an intended purpose, and without a correct understanding of our God-given purpose, we will inevitably waste our life. This is not only what many unbelievers are doing, but sadly, even many Christians across the planet today.

And yes, you can be born again, filled with the Spirit of God and still not fulfill God's purpose for your life. This is the sad reality for many believers, even myself at times. Purpose is not one climactic moment of an individual's life. Rather, our purpose is the accumulation of countless moments that we have chosen to be faithful to the Lord.

In other words, God's purpose for our life is the collection of every decision we made to honor Him throughout our life.

But, without a proper understanding of our inherent purpose, we will inevitably waste our lives and live frustrated, unfulfilled, bored, and even depressed. Why? Because when you use something in a way it wasn't intended, you accomplish nothing. And, the same rings true for our God-given breath.

Our life has an intended purpose. When we use our life for something other than it's intended purpose, there will be nothing but frustration. Don't believe me? Think of the last time you tried using something against its intended function. You probably wasted time, energy or even money which left you frustrated because you accomplished nothing. Then, when you finally figured out its intended purpose, you wish you would've known that information from the very beginning.

Nobody enjoys not knowing how to properly use something. My prayer is that by the end of this book, you'll have a fuller understanding of your God-given purpose.

The third issue we have to address is this idea of position. Before I define this word for the rest of this faith training, I have to clarify that this term only applies to Christians in the way that I'm going to use it. So, if you're not a Christian, you can change that immediately.

But, this term "position" refers to a Christian's new standing before God. In simple terms, this word refers to a Christian's identity. This is who the believer is now because of Jesus. It is how God views a believer who is positioned in Christ through faith.

Too many Christians are trying to live for God when they don't even understand how God sees them now that they're positioned in Jesus. Listen. How we think God sees us will greatly determine how we live for Him. Period. And, as Christians, we have to understand that God grants us a brand-new identity in Jesus Christ through our faith because God is gracious.

And, what I've noticed is that much of the Christian's frustration, anxiety, depression, and other related issues, are deeply rooted in the fact that they misunderstand how God sees them. Many Christians appear to be withering trees because they have deep-rooted identity issues.

Not only do many believers (myself included) have a wrong view of their identity, but, in addition, we don't understand the nature of our identity. We don't understand how this new identity functions, and how its possible for us to be who God has declared us to be.

There is a process that God divinely orchestrated to make us who we are in Christ. And, if we can better understand not only who we are, but how we are who we are, much of our internal struggles and issues will be eliminated. I'm not saying that every issue will be resolved.

And, I'm not saying that this issue of identity is the root of every problem. But, much of our emotional and mental turmoil is related to the fact that we have an identity crisis. And, by the grace of God, your sense of identity and value will be dramatically improved by the end of this book.

The last idea that we'll unpack in this faith training is our God-ordained process.

God, in His infinite wisdom, has established a process that works. This process is how God trains and transforms His people into the image of Christ in order to move His eternal plan to completion. God has a perfect strategy to accomplish His divine plan and it can't be stopped.

Think about this for a minute. God has determined a process to grow a seed into a fully-developed tree. And, that is only one example in nature. These natural processes are at work all around our universe on a daily basis.

And, just as God has put in place a process for nature, He has put a process in place for His church. There is order and structure to the ecosystem of His global body. There is an intended direction and goal that we are moving towards. He has a strategy that includes many ordered steps.

If we can align ourselves with the rhythm of God's divine process, it will make our lives much easier. I've noticed that many Christians are experiencing unnecessary difficulty simply because they're out of sync with God's divine process. I find that I'm not in step with God's pace very often, and it makes for a difficult life.

And, just like me, many believers aren't submitted to God's process. Instead, they often go against the process of God by either going after an entirely different goal or by assuming a responsibility/role that God never gave them. Sometimes we have the order wrong. Sometimes we aren't playing our role in the process. And, sometimes it can be that we misunderstand the goal of the process that God is bringing us through.

Whatever it may be, to disrupt the process of God in our life will prevent us from experiencing the fullest life possible. His divine process is perfect and it leads to the most abundant life where we are most like Jesus.

By the end of this book, you'll have a deeper understanding of God's process for your life. This is a mystery worth searching out and God has made it known in His word.

I do want to make something crystal clear before moving forward.

I'm not going to foolishly claim that every one of your problems are limited to either of these four ideas. But, for the most part, I've seen that at least one of these key issues is at the core of most troubles for believers. I don't believe God has provided a way for us to avoid every single problem in this life, because trouble is a natural consequence of this broken world.

> John 16:33 says, "**In the world you will have tribulation**. But take heart; I have overcome the world."

Clearly, troubles and problems are apart of this broken world we live in. So, the fullest Christian life is not one that has few issues. But, there are many issues that God desires for you to avoid. There are many thought patterns God intends to transform you out of. There are many addictions that God has made way for you to be free from. There are many emotional and mental troubles that God intends for you to conquer.

And, I'm convinced that whatever God has ordained for your life, specifically, this faith training will help lead you into that. God has more for you. If you want the most abundant, fruitful, God-honoring life possible, these key truths will certainly position you for that kind of life. There are levels to this training, so let's dive in.

Level 1: Purpose |

Chapter 1: Be Fruitful

God creates with purpose. Before the triune God brought our universe into existence, He had a purpose for it. The purpose for Creation came before the reality of Creation. And, what you have to understand is that we, as human beings, see our own purpose clearly within the example of the natural world around us. There's a mystery to be discovered within the purpose of our natural world. This is Level 1 of our faith training, and its important that you understand your intended purpose.

In The Beginning

In the beginning, God creates the Heavens and the Earth and He declares everything to be good. One of the reasons that it is good, is because it is fruitful. God has wired within the natural world the ability for reproduction. In other words, God enables certain created things to reproduce after their own kind. God calls it "fruitfulness."

Just like developers code their programs to accomplish a specific purpose, so God has coded this universe to function according to a specific purpose.

On the first day of Creation, God creates light and He separates that light from the darkness. On the second day, God makes the sky as a separation between the waters on earth and the waters above. But, on the third day of Creation, we see God bring something unique into existence within His ordered world.

First, God brings structure to the disorder and chaos. He does this by bringing land up out of the chaotic waters and setting boundaries that those waters cannot cross. But, then we see God create something uniquely different from everything else He's made so far. God creates something that can reproduce and make mini-versions of itself.

> *Genesis 1:11-13 tells us, "Then God said, "Let the earth bring forth grass,* **the herb that yields seed, and the fruit tree that yields fruit according to its kind, whose seed is in itself**, *on the earth"; and it was so. And the earth brought forth grass,* **the herb that yields seed according to its kind, and the tree that yields fruit, whose seed is in itself according to its kind**. *And God saw that it was good. So the evening and the morning were the third day.*

This passage tells us that God brought forth all kinds of vegetation. But, this vegetation is self-replicating. Within the DNA of vegetation, God has made reproduction possible. These "herbs" and "trees" are said to have "seed" within themselves which allow for other herbs and trees to grow outside of the original versions. We haven't seen anything like this so far in the Creation story. God has formed and structured the world but now He begins filling that container with unique creations.

Fruitful Vegetation

First, God begins with vegetation. But, this vegetation is different from the next few creations because vegetation isn't a thinking, mobile, breathing creature like animals and humans. Even so, we can't miss the point that God wires reproduction into the DNA of vegetation like the next few types of creatures. So, God makes it possible for vegetation to be "fruitful." This word is key, because it refers to reproduction which is blessed by God.

> *Genesis 1:20-23 - And God said, "Let the waters swarm with swarms of living creatures, and let birds fly above the earth across the expanse of the heavens." So God created the great sea creatures and every living creature that moves, with which the waters swarm, according to their kinds, and every winged bird according to its kind. And God saw that it was good. And* **God blessed them***, saying,* **"Be fruitful and multiply and fill the waters in the seas, and let birds multiply on the earth."** *And there was evening and there was morning, the fifth day.*

After God fills the the earth with food for the living creatures, He creates the sun, moon and stars on the fourth day. And, on the fifth day, God begins to fill the different spaces He's ordered in His world.

Sky, Water, And Land

God fills the waters with sea creatures, then He fills the expanse with sky creatures. And how does God describe these creatures? He describes them as capable of multiplying and being fruitful. How do we know this? Because He tells these sea and sky creatures to "be fruitful and multiply." Fruitfulness seems to be a theme. And, fruitfulness refers to reproduction by seed.

"Fruitfulness" has an additional element for the animals, though. God didn't command trees and herbs to reproduce. At the moment of Creation, God's word initiated the effortless process of reproduction within vegetation. But, God commands those animals in the sky and sea to reproduce and multiply.

There is a responsibility on the part of the animals to engage in sexual relations that lead to conception and reproduction. This is how these animals multiply to fill the sky and sea.

On the sixth and final day, we see God do a similar thing in creating land creatures to fill the land (earth).

> *Genesis 1:24-26 - And God said, "**Let the earth bring forth living creatures** according to their kinds—livestock and creeping things and beasts of the earth according to their kinds." And it was so. And God made the beasts of the earth according to their kinds and the livestock according to their kinds, and everything that creeps on the ground according to its kind. And God saw that it was good.*

After creating animals to fill the sea, the sky, and the earth, God commands the animal kingdom to multiply and fill the world through reproduction, which involves the seed.

In His Image

Then, we get to human beings at the end of the sixth day. And, if we know anything about God, He is a God of order, structure, and logical progression. So far, God has been creating in a certain way and with a certain purpose, and this helps us notice the natural progression in the Creation story, which ends with God creating humans in His own image.

> *Genesis 1:26-30 - Then God said, "***Let us make man in our image, after our likeness***. And let them have dominion over the fish of the sea and over the birds of the heavens and over the livestock and over all the earth and over every creeping thing that creeps on the earth."* ***So God created man in his own image, in the image of God he created him; male and female he created them.*** *And God blessed them. And God said to them, "Be fruitful and multiply and fill the earth and subdue it, and have dominion over the fish of the sea and over the birds of the heavens and over every living thing that moves on the earth." And God said, "Behold, I have given you every plant yielding seed that is on the face of all the earth, and every tree with seed in its fruit. You shall have them for food. And to every beast of the earth and to every bird of the heavens and to everything that creeps on the earth, everything that has the breath of life, I have given every green plant for food." And it was so.*

After God creates the animal kingdom, He creates human beings in His own image. He makes human beings His representatives in the earth to rule over what He created. Of course, they rule under God's authority.

So, God essentially, makes mini-versions of Himself. This doesn't mean human beings are Gods, but this does mean humans possess many attributes like God and they function on the earth as God functions over all of His creation. Humans are God's rulers on the earth who live under His protection, authority and care. We were made to oversee and cultivate the earth.

God has also declared human beings to be the best of His creation because nothing else has been made in the image of God, except humans. This is an honor. Humans have dignity, respect, value, and honor because God has uniquely made them according to His own likeness.

Then, the author of Genesis tells us that God blessed humanity. How does God bless them? The next statement makes it clear. God tells them, "be fruitful and multiply, and fill the earth and subdue it, and have dominion over the fish of the sea and over the birds of the heavens and over every living thing that moves on the earth."

So, God's blessing is found in His command. God commands humanity to be fruitful, multiply, fill the earth, and subdue the uncultivated world outside the Garden of Eden. What does it mean to "be fruitful and multiply?" It means make more human beings through sexual reproduction.

This sounds similar to what God has said to the sky, sea, and land animals, but there's an additional privilege that only humanity is given. We, human beings are on a higher level than the animals, so our purpose carries more significance.

Humanity is given charge and authority over the animal kingdom, and they are commanded to develop the earth and rule it as God's image-bearers. And, God has enabled humanity to do this. Remember, I said that God codes certain natural processes within His universe? Well, this includes humanity. God has coded humanity with the ability to multiply, so that more image-bearers of God can fill the earth.

See, part of God's blessing for humanity is found in His command. Why? Because humanity's purpose is found within God's command.

But, also, when God declares something, His word makes that reality possible now. What God declares, He makes possible. The very fact that God commands humanity to be fruitful and multiply, means it is possible for them to do so.

Ingrained into the design and DNA of humanity from the very beginning, is the ability to reproduce the image of God in the earth. By having children, humanity would be bearing fruit and multiplying the image of God just as He commanded and purposed for them.

Coded For Fruit

Humans are made to resemble a fruit tree that is bearing abundant fruit. Within the natural world is a glimpse into God's purpose for humanity.

So, for humans, being "fruitful" means replicating the image of God that they've been so graciously given. God's original design and purpose for humanity included imitation, authority, blessing, fruitfulness, and rule. This is what we see in God's original design and purpose for human beings.

God makes mankind as mini-versions of Himself and He empowers them. He loves them. He blesses them. He gives them purpose. Then, He gives them full reign, and freedom to fill the earth and develop His creation under His authority. God's original plan for us was that we would be fruitful and multiply His image.

At the time I am writing this, I've just gone to Disneyland. And, one of the areas we explored was Avengers Campus, which is the "Marvel World" within Disneyland. There's a new Spider-Man ride that involves catching runaway spider-bots that have run rampant.

These spider-bots were designed by Peter Parker to be self-replicating, which ends up becoming a huge issue. These spider-bots are coded to self-replicate, so when they duplicate themselves, they're simply functioning according to their intended purpose. They're doing what they're programmed to do.

They're coded to self-replicate, and even if it gets out of hand, the multiplication doesn't stop because its according to their program. Multiplication is in their DNA.

It is the same with human beings. Representing God is in our DNA. Bearing the image of God is programmed into our design. We are coded to bear good fruit by multiplying

Chapter 1: Be Fruitful

the image of God in the earth. This was God's intention for human beings from the very beginning. He designed human beings to be fruitful, carry His image, and multiply His image throughout the earth.

This isn't merely a physical reality, but a spiritual one as well. This idea of bearing good fruit and multiplying God's image in the earth has more spiritual implications than physical ones. Though, God did intend for this to be a physical process, there are spiritual elements to this that cannot be ignored.

Because God is Spirit, bearing His image naturally means that there is a spiritual undertone to our God-given purpose.

Before we get into these spiritual details, you just need to know that your God-given purpose is to represent God in the earth by bearing good fruit and multiplying His image.

You were made to bear good fruit like a deeply-rooted, well-watered tree. And, because this purpose of fruit-bearing carries a spiritual element, this isn't limited to physical child-bearing. For now, we have to talk about about what ruined our ability to fulfill our God-given purpose.

Level 1: Purpose |
Chapter 2: Forbidden Fruit

God created humanity to be His representatives on the earth. He created mankind to image Him by bearing good fruit and multiplying His image in the earth. So, what prevents us from accomplishing our God-given purpose? The answer is: rebellion.

When God made Adam and Eve, He not only commissioned them with a unique purpose, but He gave them a specific command to obey. This command was part of their calling. As long as they obeyed God's command, their obedience would guarantee that they'd fulfill their God-given purpose.

God didn't give them a command to restrict them or ruin their life. God gave them a command to protect them and keep them on the path of the fullest life.

Holy Guard Rails

Think of those bumpers at the bowling alley. You only put those guard rails up if you're terrible at bowling like me. But, those bumpers guarantee that your ball won't end up in the gutter.

Chapter 2: Forbidden Fruit

The same is true of God's good and holy commands. They ensure that humanity doesn't end up in the gutter of life. God's commands keep humans on the path of success, the same way the bumpers at a bowling alley keep the ball on the right path. This is God's command.

> *Genesis 2:15-17 - Then the Lord God took the man and put him in the garden of Eden to tend and keep it. And* **the Lord God commanded the man,** *saying, "Of every tree of the garden you may freely eat; but* **of the tree of the knowledge of good and evil you shall not eat**, *for in the day that you eat of it you shall surely die."*

God tells Adam that He can eat from EVERY tree in the garden except for one. There are two trees in the center of the garden of Eden. One is the tree of life and the other one is the tree of the knowledge of good and evil. Whatever stance you take on Adam And Eve's access to the tree of life, we know one thing for certain: the tree of the knowledge of good and evil was off limits. If they eat from that tree, they will die.

God's Beautiful Gift

Why would God even allow for the option of evil? Why would God be so mean and heartless? Let's talk about it.

God values love above all else. So, God creates human beings to be in a loving relationship with Him. Human beings are only able to effectively live out their God-given purpose because they are in relationship with their Creator. So, our ability to fulfill our purpose requires us to be in right relationship with God. This is the importance of love.

Real love cannot be programmed. It cannot be forced or manipulated. It cannot be manufactured. Genuine love must be freely given. Free will is required to truly love someone. And, free will means that there is the option to not love. If love is going to be a valid option, there must be another option not to love.

So, God gives human beings the beautiful gift of free will. And, the tree of knowledge of good and evil represents the choice to not love God. God said not to eat from that tree, so every time Adam and Eve walked past the tree of the knowledge of good and evil, they were choosing to love and obey God.

But, later in the story of Genesis, we discover that a spiritual being (serpent) approaches Eve and deceives her into eating the forbidden fruit. Eve ends up giving that same forbidden fruit to Adam as well, and they end up naked, exposed, and cut off from their Creator. Genesis 3:6 describes what happens when Eve gives into the temptation of the "serpent."

> Genesis 3:6 - *So when the woman saw that the tree was good for food, and that it was a delight to the eyes, and that the tree was to be desired to make one wise,* **she took of its fruit and ate, and she also gave some to her husband** *who was with her, and he ate.*

Eve gave into temptation, and ended up going against her God-given purpose. In other words, her sin was in direct violation of her God-given purpose to image God, bear fruit, and multiply the image of God in the earth. Sin always directs us away from what is best. Rebellion against God always takes us off the path of the fullest human life possible. Sin is in direct opposition to fruitfulness and it kills purpose.

But, when God told Adam and Eve that they would surely die once they rebelled, this was more than just killing their ability to fulfill their God-given purpose. Remember, we can only fulfill our purpose when we're in right relationship with God, our Creator. So, even though Adam and Eve remained physically alive, there's a certain way in which Adam and Eve "died" on the day they ate the forbidden fruit. Let me explain.

On the day that Adam and Eve rebelled against God, they experienced a spiritual death. They were cut off from their Creator God, who is the source of eternal life. God is the essence of life. He is the definition of life. And, God is the source of life. But, God declared that death was the consequence for sin. God is true to His eternal word, and Romans 6:23 affirms that death is the consequence for sinning against God.

> *Romans 6:23 - For **the wages of sin is death**, but the free gift of God is eternal life in Christ Jesus our Lord.*

According to Romans 6, the fair consequence for sin is death. What kind of death? Specifically, this refers to spiritual death, but it also includes physical death. And, spiritual death is simply separation from the God who is life.

To be cut off from the source of eternal life, means that you have no eternal life. This means that sinners are spiritually lifeless. They are dead in sin. This is why *Ephesians 2:1 says,* "***And you were dead in your trespasses and sins***" *which is referring to the old condition for the Christian.*

God's Perfect Standard

So, we have to understand that God is the one who declared that sin will naturally result in spiritual death. Adam and Eve simply met the conditions for being separated from God, but God declared this in His own perfect Law.

And, Romans 3:23 tells us that, **"all have sinned and fall short of the glory of God,"** which means that every human being is separated from God by their own sin and rebellion. There is no human being that has not sinned or failed in some way. We all miss the perfect standard of God because of sin, and we are all deserving of spiritual death.

This might seem unfair to you, but you have to understand the nature of God. He is perfectly righteous and holy. He is blameless. He is sinless. He is total perfection. God's standard is total perfection, because He is perfectly holy and righteous.

If we sin just one time, we are not perfect and we don't meet God's standard. This is a problem, because anyone who wants to dwell in the presence of God must also be perfect.

Psalm 5:4 says, *"For you are not a God who delights in wickedness;* ***evil may not dwell with you.****"*

God is so holy and perfect that no sin can dwell in His presence. Why? Because evil gets obliterated in the presence of His perfect majesty. God is so good that sin is destroyed by His goodness. Sin is incompatible with God's presence.

And, we are not good according to God's definition. Our sin taints us so that we cannot dwell in the presence of God.

Even if we only commit one sin, we fall short of God's perfect standard of righteousness because we are corrupted by evil.

*James 2:10 says, "For whoever keeps the whole law but fails in one point **has become guilty of all of it**."*

One sin makes us guilty before God. We have to understand that sin is actually crime against God, because it is a violation of His Law. Sin is high treason against the King of Kings. And, crime has consequences. There is just punishment for crime.

God has decreed that the just punishment for sin is spiritual death, because no sin can dwell in His presence. If you want to get into Heaven, you have to meet the perfect standard of God.

Many people think they're morally good, but this is only according to their own standard. In fact, most people can't even meet their own standard of moral goodness. Our own idea of "good" is something we fail to meet.

How much more do we miss God's perfect standard of righteousness? See, we utterly fail when it comes to God's perfect standard. And, God's standard is the only one that matters.

Imagine this. You're convicted of crime. You're standing before the Judge, and he has just finished reading your crimes. In response, you start to list off all of the good things you've done in order to try and escape the consequences of your crime. You finish telling the Judge why you think you're a good person, and the Judge looks at you with this confused look.

He is confused as to why you'd ever think your standard of goodness matters. He is baffled because you thought your good works could get you out of the just consequences of your crimes. He looks at you and says, "your standard of goodness doesn't matter here because you're not the Judge. And, your good works are irrelevant. You're convicted of crime here, and your good works don't change the fact that you've committed crime."

The Judge sentences you to the appropriate time in prison, and you're sent off to your prison cell. In that moment, all that mattered was the Judge's standard of goodness, and his standard of goodness came from the Law of the land. That is why you were condemned to prison. It was because you violated the Law and committed crime, and no amount of "good" deeds could make up for the crime you committed.

In the same way, our own idea of goodness really doesn't matter when it comes to getting into God's Kingdom. What matters is what the Almighty Judge says is actually good. We should be more concerned with His standard of goodness rather than our own, because He is the only one that decides whether someone enters into the Kingdom of Heaven or not. Our own perception of goodness is irrelevant when it comes to the Judge's decision about us.

And, the Judge has declared that any sin is a direct violation of His own perfect standard, and the just punishment for that crime is separation from Him forever. And, this consequence isn't only fair, but it is what the criminal desires.

Criminals sin against God because they don't want God. They don't love God, and they have no desire to include God in their life. So, God gives them what they desire, which is a reality without Him for all eternity.

Death Gains Access

Now that we've established that, I want to take you back to Genesis 3, where we see the fall of humanity.

Before Adam and Eve sin against God, there is no death within God's good world. Death wasn't apart of God's good creation.

So, how does death invade God's good world? Death had legal grounds to come into our world through human sin. And, Paul gives us some insight into this in 1 Corinthians 15.

> *1 Corinthians 15:56-57 -* **The sting of death is sin, and the power of sin is the law.** *But thanks be to God, who gives us the victory through our Lord Jesus Christ.*

According to this passage, death found access into our world through sin.

Just for a minute, let's personify death to be some dark, shadowy figure. This dark figure of death has no way to enter into our world. It isn't compatible with God's good creation, because it doesn't belong.

But, God's Law declares that death (both physical and spiritual) is the consequence for sin. And, in Genesis 3, the serpent approaches Eve knowing God's Law, so he takes advantage of the Law that God put in place. The serpent knows that God is perfect justice, so God will enforce the consequences that have been laid down by His Law.

In other words, the serpent knows that if he can get humanity to sin, then death can legally enter into God's good world through that sin. God did decree that death is the punishment for high treason against Him. And, sin is that high treason.

Death is like a poisonous spider. A spider releases its poisonous venom through its fangs, so that when a spider bites into flesh, the poison is transferred through its fangs into the victim.

In the same way, death has a "set of fangs." And, in this case, the fangs (or sting) of death is sin. Sin becomes the access point through which death inflicts its poisonous venom onto our world. God's Law declares that death has legal grounds to infect humanity through sin.

So, the serpent plays to the Law of God and death enters into our world. According to 1 Corinthians 15, the power of sin is the law. This doesn't mean God's law is the problem. Rebellious human beings are the issue. But, once again, it is God's authoritative decree that gives sin the power to legally result in death.

Now, because of our sin against a perfect, holy, righteous God, we are separated from our Creator, who is perfect love, eternal life, and absolute goodness.

We are spiritually dead because of our violation of God's Law. And, again, sin is a problem because God's righteous standard is perfection. If you want to enter into God's Kingdom you have to meet His standard of perfection, but no one can.

Everyone has sinned and owes a debt they cannot pay. Galatians 3 puts it in more helpful terms for us.

> *Galatians 3:23-24 - Now before faith came,* ***we were held captive under the law, imprisoned*** *until the coming faith would be revealed. So then,* ***the law was our guardian until Christ came****, in order that we might be justified by faith.*

Not only are we spiritually dead and separated from God by sin, but we cannot have a relationship with God because we legally belong to another master.

The Law declares that we belong to death as our legal owner. The Law holds us captive by enforcing the righteous standard of God. The Law is like a prison guard making sure that we stay in our eternal prison cell of death. The Law is just doing its job. It cannot save us, but it definitely points us to the one who can save us by exposing our sin problem.

Until we come to the one who can set us free, we are legally owned by sin, death and the devil. We are slaves to sin as Jesus says in John 8:34.

> *John 8:34 - John 8:34 - Jesus answered them, "Truly, truly, I say to you,* ***everyone who practices sin is a slave to sin****.*

This verse tells us that anyone who practices sin is a slave of sin. And, every human being sins, which means everyone one of us is a slave to sin without Jesus. But, what does this mean?

Slavery to sin refers to ownership and not control of the will. Many will say that this slavery to sin means that our will is enslaved to sin, but I believe that this refers to the fact that we are rightfully owned by sin, death and the devil by decree of God's Law.

The Law declares that we rightfully belong to sin, death and the devil as our masters. We are children of the devil, since we participate in the ways of the devil. Not only do we belong to the devil as his seed, but death is our master as well. And, there's nothing we can do about it.

On our own, we are powerless and hopeless to be set free from our oppressive masters.

Children Of The Serpent

Remember, in Genesis 3 God said the seed of the woman would be against the seed of the serpent. This means that the serpent would have "offspring" who imitate his rebellious, sinful ways. These offspring would have the same sinful nature as the serpent in the garden.

This is what it means to be a slave to sin, and this is the kind of language that Jesus uses to refer to the evil, unbelieving Jews of His day.

> John 8:44 - **You are of your father the devil, and your will is to do your father's desires**. He was a

> murderer from the beginning, and has nothing to do with the truth, because there is no truth in him. When he lies, he speaks out of his own character, for he is a liar and the father of lies.

Jesus actually says that their father is the devil, because their sinful lifestyle is a reflection of the devil. And, this is the kind of language John uses in his letter to the church.

> 1 John 3:8, 10 - **Whoever makes a practice of sinning is of the devil**, for the devil has been sinning from the beginning. The reason the Son of God appeared was to destroy the works of the devil. By this it is evident who are the children of God, and **who are the children of the devil: whoever does not practice righteousness is not of God**, nor is the one who does not love his brother.

John says that those who live in sin are children of the devil, because they have inherited his evil ways. Think of the kind of fruit that falls off of an apple tree. Only apples can come from an apple tree, and this means that apples carry the seed to produce more apple trees.

You might want something else, but an apple seed that comes from an apple tree is only capable of giving you apples. It inherits the traits of the tree it comes from.

This is the same "seed" language used of those who live in sin as the devil, or the serpent does in the garden. It means the ways of the devil have passed onto us through the sinful nature we have inherited from Adam.

We might want to be something else, but we cannot change the sinful nature we have inherited from Adam. Adam chose to imitate the sinful ways of the serpent, and so does the rest of humanity without Jesus.

But, in 1 John 3, the children of God are contrasted with the children of the devil, because true children of God have repented of sin and turned to Jesus in faith. And, this assumes they recognize sin as something they no longer want to participate in.

Ephesians 2 puts it another way, to give us a clearer picture of humanity without Jesus. And, I hope this shows you what we were before we trusted in Jesus for salvation.

> *Ephesians 2:1-3 - And you were dead in the trespasses and sins in which you once walked, following the course of this world, following the prince of the power of the air, the spirit that is now at work in the sons of disobedience– among whom we all once lived in the passions of our flesh, carrying out the desires of the body and the mind, and* **were by nature children of wrath, like the rest of mankind**.

Paul describes human beings apart from Jesus as being sons of disobedience, children of wrath, dead in sin, following the ways of this sinful world, and following the dark spiritual powers in the world. These are key descriptors that we should meditate on if we want to fully understand why humanity is helpless without Jesus.

Chapter 2: Forbidden Fruit

Remember, this all relates to the fact that we not only were separated from God, but we were also robbed of our ability to fulfill our God-given purpose.

Our sinful nature didn't fit the purpose that God had for us. Because our sinful nature wasn't compatible with our designed purpose, we weren't able to accomplish that purpose. Let me revisit the fruit analogy for a minute.

An apple tree is designed to produce apples, but if you want grapes, you'll have to find an entirely different fruit. The DNA of apple seeds isn't capable of fulfilling the purpose that grape seeds were designed for.

This is an illustration of what we were without Christ. We were made for a purpose that wasn't compatible with our inherited, sinful nature.

This doesn't mean that human beings were not able to image God anymore. This just means that apart from Jesus, we are not able to image God honorably and faithfully. Human beings are God's image in the earth, so we can't stop imaging God.

But, that image has been tarnished and ruined by sin, so now, our sinfulness obstructs the glory of God from being seen in our lives. We need a new nature in order to image God well.

Let's go back to Ephesians 2. Paul said that before we came to Jesus, we were dead in sin, which means we were cut off from God.

Paul also says that we once followed the course (or direction) of this world. This world system is going the opposite direction of God, because it is being guided by the spiritual forces of darkness. And, we once were puppets for the evil spiritual forces.

We did whatever felt good, seemed good, and looked good, which was leading us towards hell along with the rest of the unbelieving world. In other words, we submitted our lives to the powers of darkness, so that they could accomplish their dark agenda through our lives. The devil was leading our lives at one point, because we were deceived.

The last description Paul uses of unbelieving humans is that they were children of wrath. This carries the same idea of being children (or seed) of the devil, but Paul adds another layer to it.

Because we were on the side of the evil rebels, we were under the sentence of God's wrath. There was one ultimate destiny for us: separation from God under His righteous wrath. God's just, righteous wrath was what we earned by living in sin.

Picture a ship in the ocean that is heading right for a massive, destructive whirlpool. Those on the ship don't know they're headed right towards it but, because of the course they chose, but they're headed towards inevitable death.

There is no way out for these people. They can do nothing about it. But, all of their previous navigational decisions are what led them to this moment of doom. This is a picture of us before Christ came and saved us from eternal death. We were helplessly on a one-way track towards hell because of the course decisions we had made by sinning.

In fact, Ephesians 2:12 speaks of this hopeless, inevitable death we were headed towards.

> *Ephesians 2:12 - remember that* **you were at that time separated from Christ**, *alienated from the commonwealth of Israel and strangers to the covenants of promise,* **having no hope and without God in the world**.

This passage is reminding Ephesian Gentiles that they were once hopeless, cut off from Jesus, and without God in the world.

This wasn't just true of Gentiles, but even unbelieving Jews. All people have sinned against an infinitely holy God, and are therefore, hopelessly separated from God, waiting for inevitable eternal death. But, all of that changes with Jesus.

Level 1: Purpose |
Chapter 3: Promised Seed

In Genesis 3, God makes a very important promise to humanity. This promise is the first glimpse into the beautiful news of the gospel message. Adam and Eve have just sinned against God, after being deceived by the serpent, and now they're cut off from their Creator God because of their rebellion.

Humanity is rendered incapable of fully accomplishing their God-given purpose as a result of being separated from God. Their ability to image God has been disrupted because their relationship with God has been ruined.

But, the promise of God in Genesis 3 gives humanity unspeakable hope.

> *Genesis 3:14-15 - The Lord God said to the serpent, "Because you have done this, cursed are you above all livestock and above all beasts of the field; on your belly you shall go, and dust you shall eat all the days of your life. And I will put enmity Between you and the woman, And between your seed and her Seed;* **He shall bruise your head, And you shall bruise His heel.**"

God promises that a chosen future descendent (a seed) would eventually come through Eve, and this "seed" would crush the head of the serpent. I want you to pay special attention to this word "seed" that God chooses to use, as this idea carries several dimensions that we have to explore to make sense of everything we're going to discuss later in this book.

This "seed" language refers not just to a future descendent that would come from the woman, but it links back to the original purpose for which God designed humanity. He designed them to be fruitful and multiply, which included having children to fill the earth.

Remember, just as a tree carries seed to produce more trees, so God has coded humans to possess "seed" that has potential to produce more image-bearers through the right process.

I want to emphasize this term "seed," because we will be using this same terminology all throughout this book.

The Chosen One

But, first, we have to establish who this "promised seed" is, and what it means that He crushes the head of the serpent. Then, from there we can make sense of how He is the greatest, most divine gift for humanity who restores both our relationship with God and our purpose.

The entire Biblical story is centered around this promised seed, or chosen one. The New Testament reveals this chosen one fully, while the Old Testament is predicting this chosen one, anticipating Him, and preparing humanity for His coming.

There are glimpses and shadows of this chosen one throughout the Old Testament, but He isn't fully revealed until the New Testament.

The Old Testament is mostly about God's divine plan to bring this chosen one into our world to save us. God uses several chosen individuals to give birth to a chosen nation, and through this chosen nation, the chosen one would fulfill the promise that God made in Genesis 3.

John 3:16 tells us exactly who this chosen "seed" is.

> John 3:16 - For God so loved the world, that **he gave his only Son**, that whoever believes in him should not perish but have eternal life.

This chosen seed that God promised to bring into the world was His precious Son, Jesus Christ of Nazareth. This is the Jewish carpenter born in Bethlehem to redeem humanity and restore us back to the Father.

God gave us the gift of His eternally loved, divine Son. And, this Jesus was not one among many. This Jesus was God's ONLY Son.

This divine Son of God would sacrifice His own life willingly, in order to accomplish more than we could ever imagine. What we're about to see is that this chosen one didn't simply restore humanity back to the position that we fell from. Jesus restores us to something even better.

Chapter 3: Promised Seed

It would be one thing for God to simply restore us to where we fell from. But, He goes above and beyond what we could ever ask, think or imagine.

Our limited human minds would've never imagined to ask for what God has given us. Our tiny, human minds don't possess the ability to even conceive of what God has done for us through His precious Son. In other words, what God has given us, is something only His infinite mind could've dreamed up.

But, what exactly has Jesus, the Jewish carpenter from Nazareth, accomplished for humanity? He has done exactly what was promised in Genesis 3. Jesus has crushed the head of the serpent, which means He has conquered the powers of darkness that once conquered us.

He has victoriously triumphed over all of our enemies, but how has Jesus done this?

> 1 John 3:8 says, "The reason the Son of God appeared was to **destroy the works of the devil**."

John tells us that Jesus has destroyed the works of the devil. This is one way to explain the fact that Jesus has crushed the head of the serpent. But, there are many dimensions to this.

We have to remember who we're enslaved to, in order to make sense of what Jesus has done.

Humanity is enslaved to three main masters. These are the big three: sin, death and the devil. So, whatever Jesus has done to destroy the works of the devil, and crush the head of the serpent, He has set us free from all three of these evil masters.

And, the law is a part of this as well, but the law is not evil. The law is good. We are evil and cannot meet the standard of God's Law because of our own wicked heart. The Law of God just functions as the legal aspect of this entire situation we're in.

Whatever Jesus does, He deals with the Law, our sin, our death, and consequently, He deals with the devil. But, what we have to understand is that Jesus has to be one of us in order to legally set us free from our masters. This is what Paul teaches in Galatians 4 about Jesus.

> Galatians 4:4-7 - But when the fullness of time had come, **God sent forth his Son, born of woman, born under the law, to redeem those who were under the law, so that we might receive adoption as sons.** And because you are sons, God has sent the Spirit of his Son into our hearts, crying, "Abba! Father!" So you are no longer a slave, but a son, and if a son, then an heir through God.

In order for human beings to bet set free from their slavery and restored back to God, Jesus has to come as a human being under the same Law that we are under. In other words, Jesus steps into our prison cell with us. And, He doesn't intend to stay in there.

Chapter 3: Promised Seed

One Of Us

Remember, Galatians 3 says that we were held captive under the Law, imprisoned, waiting for Jesus to come and set us free. And, Jesus comes into His own created world. He takes on human flesh, He plays by His own rules, and He accomplishes the victory that we could never have achieved on our own.

It is human beings who have sinned against God, and therefore it is humans who are deserving of spiritual death. This is why Jesus has to come as a human being. But, this doesn't mean Jesus is merely another human. He is also God. And, He had to be God for a couple of very important reasons. Let's first look at the significance of Jesus coming into our broken world as a human.

> *Hebrews 2:17-18 -* **Therefore he had to be made like his brothers in every respect**, *so that he might become a merciful and faithful high priest in the service of God,* **to make propitiation for the sins of the people.** *18 For because he himself has suffered when tempted, he is able to help those who are being tempted.*

The author of life, had to take on human nature in order to be the perfect sacrifice for humanity's sins. If Jesus is going to restore us back to a relationship with God, this means He will be acting as a bridge. And, this is why the author of Hebrews says Jesus is our High Priest.

Hebrews teaches that Jesus is our great High Priest. Without getting too deep into the Old Testament, this just means that

Jesus stands before God the Father on our behalf, so that He can function as the bridge between man and God.

In the Old Testament, it was the High Priest who would stand before God in the Holy of Holies, which was located in the most sacred part of the temple in Jerusalem. This High Priest would perform certain rituals on the day of Atonement, which was only once a year.

God prescribed these rituals to be done in order for His presence to continue dwelling among the people of Israel. This High Priest would stand before God to represent the Israelite nation and perform certain sacrifices and rituals on their behalf.

Why does God command these specific rituals? God is an infinitely holy God who was dwelling among evil, sinful Israelites. These Israelites needed their uncleanness to be dealt with, so that God could dwell among them. And, God commanded animal sacrifices that would handle the ritual uncleanness of the people throughout the year. This was always a kind of temporary reset for the people of Israel.

This Day of Atonement was only once a year, and the High Priest had the most important role on that day to handle the uncleanness of the Israelite nation. You might think God is conceited for requiring such an intense ritual system so that His presence could dwell among the people of Israel. And, I used to think that too.

In fact, I used to ask, "Why does God require blood to atone for sin?" That seems a bit dark. But, then I remembered that Psalm 5:4 tells us that sin cannot dwell in the presence of the

Chapter 3: Promised Seed

Almighty God. He is too good for sin to dwell in His presence. His righteous holiness obliterates anything tainted with sin.

So, evil has to be dealt with in order for a human to dwell in close proximity to His presence. And, I've always wondered, "why does God required blood, though?" And, the answer is found in Leviticus 17:11.

> Leviticus 17:11 - **For the life of the flesh is in the blood**, and I have given it for you on the altar to make atonement for your souls, for **it is the blood that makes atonement by the life**.

This passage teaches us that the life of a creature is in its blood. And, death is the penalty of sin, which means sin legally demands the life of the sinner. Sin results in loss of life. So, blood is what makes atonement for sin, because the life is wrapped up in the blood of a creature.

In the Old Testament, God had His people make animal sacrifices so that their unintentional sin and uncleanness could be temporarily dealt with each year. But, there was always need for another animal sacrifice, which means these sacrifices were offered repeatedly.

Animal blood was never valuable or sufficient enough to pay for sin and cleanse a person fully in the sight of God. This animal blood was pointing to a more precious blood that would be spilled to deal with all of humanity's sin once and for all. Animal blood was never enough to completely cleanse the heart and conscience of a person, but it was a temporary fix until an ultimate sacrifice would eventually come.

So, Jesus comes into our world to act as our ultimate High Priest and sacrifice for sin. He would be the one to approach God the Father on our behalf, with His own sacrificial blood that could fully pay for humanity's crimes. But, Jesus also had to be sinless, just as temple animal sacrifices had to be without blemish. This is what Hebrews 4 teaches.

> Hebrews 4:15 - *For we do not have a high priest who is unable to sympathize with our weaknesses, but one who **in every respect has been tempted as we are, yet without sin**.*

The author of Hebrews tells us that Jesus was tempted in every possible way, yet He remained without sin. Just as we are tempted by sin, Jesus had to be tempted completely if He was really going to be the perfect human in our place. Jesus didn't skip the hard parts of humanity. When He came into this broken world, He experienced everything that we do, which includes temptation.

But, if Jesus is going to represent us before God the Father and become the bridge between God and man, He had to be the perfect human being that everyone has failed to be. He couldn't sin even once. And, Hebrews tells us that Jesus never failed. He committed zero sin throughout His life on earth, whether in His actions, speech, heart, thoughts, or attitudes.

Jesus was perfect and without fault. That sounds impossible, because we only know of broken humans who have failed. We don't know anyone who has never once sinned. We don't know of any human being who has perfectly embodied love and holiness every moment of their life. But, Jesus has.

Chapter 3: Promised Seed

I know all of these details sound unimportant, and even boring for some, but every one of these ideas connects to your purpose and your new future in Christ. In other words, your ability to fulfill your God-given purpose is directly related to every one of these crucial details. Don't miss it.

Remember, God's Law is His perfect standard that we fall short of. We can't enter into His Kingdom because we fall short of His perfect standard. Therefore, someone has to meet the perfect standard of God on our behalf, if they're going to represent us before the Father. This is exactly what Jesus says He does.

> *Matthew 5:17 - "Do not think that I have come to abolish the Law or the Prophets; I have not come to abolish them **but to fulfill them**.*

Jesus says that He fulfills the Law of God, and the Prophets, which is the entire Old Testament. Jesus is claiming to be the substance and fulfillment of the entire Old Testament. The Old Testament finds its meaning and completion in Jesus. Think of the Old Testament like a container that Jesus is filling up to the full.

Jesus not only fulfills the perfect standard of God by living perfect, but He does so much more. He fulfills every prophecy made about Him. He is the perfect image of what every Old Testament character failed to be. He brings meaning and substance to every promise given by God in the Old Testament. Every promise of God is yes and amen in Christ.

So, when I say that Jesus fulfilled His own perfect standard in our place, I mean so much more than just following His own rules.

But, Jesus does play by His own rules. He doesn't bypass the Law. He came under our Law in order to do what no other human ever could. He lives the perfect, sinless human life. And, you can't miss this. The perfect life of Jesus is what enables Him to effectively conquer our three masters of sin, death and the devil.

So, how does Jesus set us free by living as the perfect human we failed to be? Jesus is eventually condemned to death by crucifixion. He is brutally scourged, tortured, He is given a crown of thorns which symbolizes the curse of sin, and He is nailed to a wooden cross where He suffers to the point of death.

On that wooden cross, as Jesus is suffering beyond belief, something divine is taking place. This crucifixion was according to the plan of God to bring salvation to humanity. Sin had to be dealt with for humanity to be set free from death and the devil, and God deals with sin in a way that no one saw coming.

> *2 Corinthians 5:21 -* **For He made Him who knew no sin to be sin for us**, *that we might become the righteousness of God in Him.*

2 Corinthians 5 tells us that Jesus became the embodiment of sin on that wooden cross. He became the essence of our spiritual darkness and sin, in order to accomplish a

divine exchange for humanity. Jesus takes our death, and we receive His life.

And, these are two questions I've always had:

1) How can this happen?
2) Why does Jesus have to become our sin?

Romans 8:3-4 - For God has done what the law, weakened by the flesh, could not do. By sending his own Son in the likeness of sinful flesh and for sin, **he condemned sin in the flesh,** *4* **in order that the righteous requirement of the law might be fulfilled in us,** *who walk not according to the flesh but according to the Spirit.*

We've already established that God's Law was never intended to save us. It was always designed to expose our sin problem and then point us to Jesus who saves us. So, Jesus does what the Law never could. He saves us by obeying the Law perfectly in order to be the perfect, blameless sacrifice we needed.

And, that holy, blameless Son of God becomes our sin for a very specific reason.

Remember, our sin deserves just penalty, which is death, or separation from God. Because of sin, we deserve to be condemned to eternal death. So, there is a debt we owe because of our crime. And, Jesus has paid our debt fully by willingly laying down His life for us.

He becomes our sin, so that He can be punished instead of us. On that cross, every ounce of the punishment that we deserve is poured out onto Jesus. He is penalized in our place, as the embodiment of our spiritual darkness. Sin is condemned and punished fully in the flesh of Jesus.

How does Jesus satisfy the just penalty of our sin? Besides the physical torture, humiliation, and shame, Jesus is spiritually separated from the Father, in a way that He has never known. The Law declares that we are separated from God by our sin, so Jesus steps in our place and is separated from the Father temporarily, so that we never have to be separated from God.

God In The Flesh

Jesus has always, eternally co-existed with God the Father and The Spirit in perfect love, unity, harmony, and agreement. He has always been God the Son alongside God the Father and The Spirit. This is what John 1 declares about Jesus.

> *John 1:1-4 - In the beginning was the Word, and the Word was with God, and* **the Word was God. 2 He was in the beginning with God.** *3 All things were made through him, and without him was not any thing made that was made. 4 In him was life, and the life was the light of men.*

Jesus is the Word, who has always existed in eternity past alongside God the Father, but He is also God. This doesn't mean He is a separate deity. This means that He is perfectly, co-equally God alongside the Father and the Holy Spirit.

He shares the same divine essence and nature of the Father so that He is complete deity just as the Father and Holy Spirit.

Chapter 3: Promised Seed

The Father, Son and Spirit are three distinct persons that compose one divine being. They are each individual persons who are not each other, but share the same divine essence as one triune God.

And, I bring this point up, because Jesus can only satisfy the just penalty for humanity's sin if He is both man and God. And, this is what the Bible teaches very clearly from Genesis to Revelation.

Scripture reveals that Jesus is completely God and completely man. He is full divinity veiled in human flesh. And, this makes the work of Jesus even more significant for us. It would be one thing if another human died for us, but it is an entirely different thing to know that the eternal God of Heaven has chosen to come into our broken world as one of us in order to die in our place.

This is why Philippians 2 is such an important passage for understanding the beauty of the gospel message.

> *Philippians 2:5-7 - Have this mind among yourselves, which is yours in Christ Jesus,* **6** *who, though* **he was in the form of God**, *did not count equality with God a thing to be grasped,* **7 but emptied himself, by taking the form of a servant, being born in the likeness of men**.

Jesus is said to have been in the form of God, which means He had the substance and nature of God. The word "form" refers to both His humanity and divinity in this passage. He is deity. He is God. And, as God, He is entitled to so much.

He is worthy and deserving of infinitely more than we can comprehend.

Yet, even though He had divine entitlements, He chose to fill a human body with His divine essence in order to lay down His life and die the death we deserve. He became everything we needed as the perfect, divine human. He left His eternal glory to suffer a shameful death.

If Jesus is going to pay for all of humanity's sin and satisfy the wrath of God, He has to be God in the flesh. Many Christians have no idea why this is such an important teaching of Christianity, so here is why it matters that we believe Jesus is God.

The nature of our punishment is endless. When a sinner dies, they aren't separated from God for a while. They're separated forever. The nature of our punishment is infinite. So, the sacrifice for humanity's sin has to be infinite in order to absorb the infinite punishment for humanity's crime, which is the infinite wrath of God.

Not only that, but the sacrifice for humanity has to be eternal, which means that this sacrifice must have no beginning and no end. Every human being that has ever lived has sinned.

Since the beginning of time, all throughout human history, every human has sinned. And, in the Old Testament, there are saints who are saved through their faith in the God of Israel. But, Jesus hadn't died yet, so how is there a sacrifice for their sin? The answer is: Jesus' sacrifice applies to every human being across time.

But, that isn't the way sacrifices are supposed to work. Usually, a sacrifice only applies to those who are alive during the time the sacrifice is made.

In the Old Testament, animal sacrifices didn't apply to dead Israelites or Israelites who hadn't been born yet. They only benefitted those who were alive during the time of that sacrifice. So, animal sacrifices were limited in the sense that they only applied to those currently alive.

How is Jesus then able to pay for the sins of all humanity?

Because Jesus exists at every point in human history. Jesus has no beginning or end. He has always existed eternally and He will always exists eternally outside of time. So, Jesus exists at every point in human history where sin was committed.

Being the eternal God, He is able to pay for all sin across all time, because His life spans all of human history. His sacrifice doesn't only apply to those who were alive during the time of His death. His sacrifice applies to every human being who has ever lived.

Jesus pays for every sin every committed, because His precious blood is infinitely valuable. His life is more than sufficient enough to satisfy the just penalty for all sin. His death and resurrection signal the end of sin's tyranny and oppression of humanity.

Crushing Old Masters

This is how Jesus deals with our sin and our spiritual death that we deserve. Jesus dies our death so that we can have

His eternal life. Jesus doesn't come into our spiritual prison to comfort us in it. He enters into our spiritual prison cell to kick the doors down from the inside so that we can be free from sin and death.

This is exactly what Galatians 3:23-24 teaches. The Law of God declared that we rightly belonged to sin, death and the devil. We were slaves. So, before we could be restored back to God, we had to be set free from our old masters.

This is where the resurrection of Jesus is key to understanding our salvation and relationship with God. The bible tells us that Jesus died on the cross, but three days later He resurrected back to life in the power of God to demonstrate that He possesses power over death.

Death cannot contain Jesus. He decided when He would die and He decided when He would rise again. If Jesus stays dead, we are still hopelessly dead in sin. But, Jesus has come back to life in order to gain back everything humanity lost in Genesis 3.

Jesus' triumph on the cross wasn't a victory that He needed. He is God, so He needs nothing, because He lacks nothing. This wasn't about Jesus gaining a victory He didn't already possess. His death and resurrection as the perfect human, was to win back the power and authority humanity forfeited in Genesis 3.

But, He had to die as our sin, so that we could die to our old sinful life and be raised to life as a new creation in Christ. Galatians 2 puts it this way.

Chapter 3: Promised Seed

Galatians 2:19-20 - For **through the law I died to the law, so that I might live to God. I have been crucified with Christ. It is no longer I who live, but Christ who lives in me**. *And the life I now live in the flesh I live by faith in the Son of God, who loved me and gave himself for me.*

Our old sinful life had to be done away with, because that old life belonged to sin, death and the devil. So, Jesus' resurrection is what enables us to be raised to life with Him. We are given brand new lives that Jesus paid for with His blood. We couldn't legally be adopted by God as His children, until our debt was paid, and our old masters were removed.

Romans 7:1-4 gives us a helpful analogy in understanding this divine transaction that took place through Jesus' precious blood.

Romans 7:1-4 - Or do you not know, brothers—for I am speaking to those who know the law—that the law is binding on a person only as long as he lives? ***2*** *For a married woman is bound by law to her husband while he lives, but if her husband dies she is released from the law of marriage.* ***3*** *Accordingly, she will be called an adulteress if she lives with another man while her husband is alive. But if her husband dies, she is free from that law, and if she marries another man she is not an adulteress.* ***4*** **Likewise, my brothers, you also have died to the law through the body of Christ, so that you may belong to another**, *to him who has been raised from the dead, in order that we may bear fruit for God.*

The marriage covenant between a man and a woman is only active as long as both individuals are alive. But, once one of them dies, the other living person is free to marry someone else, because that covenant is no longer active.

The marriage covenant is active until someone dies. This is how it is with us. The Law declared us guilty of sin, condemned to hell, and separated from God with no way out. This was the old agreement between man and God before Jesus came.

But, Jesus establishes a new agreement between man and God. If someone should trust in His death and resurrection for forgiveness and salvation, that person will die to the old agreement. After dying to their old life, they will be born again by the Holy Spirit as a new person that can rightfully belong to God. And, all of this takes place through our faith.

This is the divine method God has put in place. God makes way for our salvation and He chooses to save us because He is gracious. But, the way He saves us is through our faith in His Son. We are saved through faith, by God's grace. Grace is simply the kindness and favor of God, that we do not deserve. It is unearned, undeserved, and unmerited. It is His free gift.

> Ephesians 2:8-10 - For **by grace** you have been saved through faith. And this is not your own doing; **it is the gift of God**, *9* not a result of works, so that no one may boast.

We are saved through our faith in Jesus who has made way for our salvation. Period. Jesus has signed our adoption

Chapter 3: Promised Seed

papers with His precious blood, and we either trust in Him to get us back to the Father or we don't.

His death and resurrection makes way for us to be able to die to our old lives in order to be raised to life as a child of God who has been adopted by The Father. This adoption is only possible, because Jesus signed our adoption papers with His invaluable blood.

This is what God promised in Genesis 3. He promised that the chosen one would come to restore us back to Him and win back everything humanity lost through their sin. Jesus is the only way to have a living relationship with God. This is what He says in John 14.

> *John 14:6 - Jesus said to him, "I am the way, and the truth, and the life.* **No one comes to the Father except through me.**

There is only one path back to the Father and it is through believing and trusting in Jesus who has made a way back to the Father. Only one person has lived the perfect life we never could. One person has paid our debt and died our death so that we could have His eternal life; Jesus Christ the promised seed.

We can actually have eternal life now because someone else paid for it with His precious blood. And, this is how Jesus defines "eternal life."

> *John 17:3 - And* **this is eternal life**, *that they know you, the only true God, and Jesus Christ whom you have sent.*

According to this passage, eternal life is knowing God the Father through Jesus, the divine Son. Eternal life isn't simply living forever. It is living forever in the perfect presence of God.

Eternal life is possessing a real relationship with the triune God. Now, through Jesus, we are adopted as children of God, filled with His Holy Spirit, and forever welcome into the presence of God. Jesus has restored us back to God through our faith in Him and He has filled us with His very Spirit.

But, what about the devil? I know you're probably thinking I forgot about that last master; the devil. How did Jesus deal with him? Well, Jesus stripped the devil of his power and authority when He resurrected from the grave on our behalf. He won back the eternal life that we forfeited through our sin and rebellion.

When Jesus conquered death and sin, He was also triumphing over the devil and the powers of darkness. In Ephesians 2, Paul speaks of God's power that was demonstrated through Jesus' resurrection. He tells us how Jesus conquered the powers of darkness on our behalf.

> *Ephesians 2:20-23 - that he worked in Christ when he raised him from the dead and seated him at his right hand in the heavenly places,* **21** *far above all rule and authority and power and dominion, and above every name that is named, not only in this age but also in the one to come.* **22** *And he put all things under his feet and gave him as head over all things to the church,* **23** *which is his body, the fullness of him who fills all in all.*

Chapter 3: Promised Seed

After Jesus resurrected from the dead, He eventually ascended back into Heaven to sit at the right hand of the throne of God the Father. Jesus is there to represent us before the Father as our great High Priest. His precious blood is what allows us to enter into God's presence. And, He sits there as the perfect human one, who has been exalted to a place that is far above all spiritual powers and names of authority.

The authority that Jesus has been given as the perfect human, is infinitely above any spiritual power and ruler that exists. These evil spiritual forces and dark rulers are placed under the power and authority of Jesus, who has been exalted to that position of power for our benefit.

He has always been the infinitely powerful God who possesses all authority. He has always been above everything. But, we possessed no power or authority over the powers of darkness.

So, now Jesus sits at the right hand of the Father as the perfect human one. He possesses divine, human authority over all dark spiritual forces. In other words, He's won back what Adam and Eve forfeited in the garden of Eden. He is in authority for our good, and in our place, so that we inherit that same power through our faith.

When Adam and Eve sinned, they forfeited the authority and rulership of the earth that God had granted them. Now, through their sin, they gave the devil and his demons legal power and authority over them. The devil once had power and authority over humanity through our sin. But, Jesus broke the spiritual chains that were over humanity, so that anyone who would trust in His name for salvation would have authority over the devil and his demons.

The devil and the powers of darkness no longer have any legal claim on children of God who believe in Jesus for salvation. Jesus' victory is ours, His reward is ours, and His life is ours, because we inherit these things through our faith. God has declared that Jesus' victory and reward is ours by faith.

Did you notice the language Paul used in Ephesians 2? It sounds very similar to the language God uses in Genesis 3 about the promised seed. Paul says that all things (including, and especially the spiritual forces of darkness) have been placed under the feet of Jesus.

Jesus is in a position of power above all existing rule and authority. He is the ultimate power and the final authority, not just as God, but also as the perfect human. Everything is beneath the feet of Jesus. He is the unstoppable one.

This brings us back to the original promise that God made in Genesis 3.

Remember, God says that the seed of the woman would crush the head of the serpent. And, yes this promise is primarily about Jesus. He is the One who crushes the head of the serpent, through His death and resurrection. This is exactly what Paul says Jesus accomplished through His resurrection and ascension.

Paul is telling us plainly that Jesus has accomplished an eternal victory over the devil, and this is for the benefit of humanity.

But, in Genesis 3, we're told that the seed of the serpent (plural) would be at odds with the seed of the woman, and this seed of the woman includes more than just Jesus. Anyone who has believing loyalty in Jesus, is made a child of God. They're made royalty because they inherit Jesus' exalted human position. In other words, Jesus came down to our level, in order to bring us up to His.

This doesn't mean we are Gods (or gods). This simply means that we are royal children of God who get to inherit the rewards and victory of our Savior.

Again, Jesus' victory is our own. We conquer through His triumph. Ephesians tells us that we are now positioned in Jesus through our faith. So, if He is above all spiritual forces of darkness, then so are we. This conquering language does't only apply to Jesus, but it applies to those who trust in His blood for forgiveness.

So, In Genesis 3, when it says the "seed" of the woman would crush the head of the serpent, this includes anyone who would seek refuge in the ultimate promised seed.

Through Christ, God's promises to His people now apply to us. We are born again of the Spirit, adopted as children of God into His royal family, so that now we're in a position of triumph alongside Jesus. This is what Paul says in Romans 16.

> *Romans 16:20 - The God of peace **will soon crush Satan under your feet**. The grace of our Lord Jesus Christ be with you.*

Who is crushing satan under their feet? Paul says this is referring to Christians. But, our victory over spiritual darkness is only possible because of Christ's ultimate victory over sin, death and the devil.

Notice that Paul says God "will soon" crush satan under our feet. Though, we are currently in a place of total triumph, there is a future victory we are waiting for when Jesus returns. He will completely remove the devil and his demons for good.

So, right now the devil and the powers of darkness are under Christ's feet as well as our own. We have victory now. But, Hebrews 10 speaks of the full experience of this victory one day.

> *Hebrews 10:12-13 - But when Christ had offered for all time a single sacrifice for sins, he sat down at the right hand of God,* **13** *waiting from that time* ***until his enemies should be made a footstool for his feet***.

We are waiting for the day where we see the full revelation of Jesus' victory made reality. Jesus is sitting in Heaven pleading our case before the Father as the perfect defense attorney, but He's also waiting to return in power at His second coming.

And, when He comes, He won't be coming as the sacrificial lamb to be slain. He'll be coming as the roaring lion who executes perfect vengeance and justice on His enemies. This is the day we're waiting for.

Jesus will obliterate death. He will completely remove the reality of sin. And, He will absolutely annihilate the devil and his demons once and for all.

Chapter 3: Promised Seed

But, until then, what do we do? While we're waiting for Judgment Day when everything will be made right, how can we be preparing for eternity in God's presence? What does God want us to be doing now on earth? How do we fully live out our God-given purpose?

These are questions we should be asking, and the rest of this book will be dedicated to answering them in depth. Trust me, it only gets better from here.

Level 1: Purpose |
Chapter 4: Fruit Defined

Throughout the last three chapters, we discov-ered that God created humanity to image Him. We image God when we bear good fruit and multiply His image in the earth. When God told Adam and Eve to be fruitful and multiply, He was indicating that humanity's purpose is primarily about bearing good fruit.

I don't want to over-simplify our purpose by restricting it to one simple concept, but we exist to image God faithfully, which involves bearing good fruit.

Jesus says it this way in *John 15:8, "By this my Father is glorified,* **that you bear much fruit** *and so prove to be my disciples."* Apparently, God is glorified when His people bear much fruit because this proves they are true disciples of Jesus.

But, what does this even mean? This idea can be defined many different ways, so we have to be careful to define this idea precisely and biblically. If you don't accurately define this idea of bearing good fruit, you'll end up spending your life on something God never said to pursue.

So, for the sake of walking out our God-given purpose, let's examine a few Scriptures that make sense of what it means to bear good fruit.

> Romans 7:4 tells us, "*Likewise, my brothers, you also have died to the law through the body of Christ, so that you may belong to another, to him who has been raised from the dead,* **in order that we may bear fruit for God**."

Romans 7 is telling us that Jesus not only restored our relationship with God, but He has also restored our ability to produce good fruit for God.

As we saw in the last chapter, sin disrupted our ability to produce good fruit and image God faithfully. Sin ruined our capacity to accomplish our God-ordained purpose. This is one of the reasons we had to be set free from our old masters through the death and resurrection of King Jesus.

So, bearing good fruit for God, is the natural result of being set free from the penalty sin. Now that we belong to God, good fruit is possible. Our closeness with God enables fruitfulness in our lives.

Restored Connection

Think of how WiFi works with your laptop. Most laptops requires WIFI in order to access the internet. The closer you are to the source of the WiFi, the stronger your connection is to the internet, and the faster your internet speed will be.

If you have a laptop that requires a WiFi source, you cannot access the internet on that laptop if you're not close enough to the source of the WiFi. Your laptop has the ability to go online and do many different things on the internet, but if you are out of range from a local WiFi connection, your laptop's internet capabilities become useless. But, once you're in the range of a local WiFi hotspot, your laptop's online capabilities are activated.

In the same way, human beings have the ability to image God and bear good fruit, but that ability is deactivated as long as we're separated from God because of sin. That ability is not functional without a relationship with God, because He powers that ability.

But, the minute we're raised to life through faith in Christ, we're born again to a living relationship with God, and our fruit-bearing ability is activated. Now, we are able to bear good fruit simply because we have a restored connection with God. That connection enables us to bear good fruit.

Romans 7 actually teaches that without a relationship with God, it is impossible to bear good fruit that glorifies Him. He is the One who enables good fruit in our lives.

1 John 3:9 gives us some more insight into this idea.

> *1 John 3:9 - No one born of God makes a practice of sinning, for **God's seed abides in him**, and **he cannot keep on sinning** because he has been born of God.*

Notice how John uses the word "seed" to refer to what abides in a true child of God. I believe this "seed" mainly

Chapter 4: Fruit Defined

refers to the Spirit of God who dwells within us. But, this can also include the seed of the gospel that was planted in our hearts through faith.

It is the Spirit of God that will effectively produce change in our lives. And, if we're thinking about fruit, we have to remember that seed comes before fruit.

Seed is planted in us, in order to produce the good fruit that God desires. Fruit comes from seed. So, the message of the gospel should produce noticeable change in our lives, and it is the Spirit of God who accomplishes the production of that fruit.

I want you to see that good fruit is naturally produced through the "seed" God has planted in us, and it is only possible because of our newly-restored connection to God. But, there is one more passage of Scripture that helps us make sense of this idea as it relates to our purpose.

> *1 Peter 1:22-25 - Having purified your souls by your obedience to the truth for a sincere brotherly love, love one another earnestly from a pure heart, since you have been born again,* **not of perishable seed but of imperishable, through the living and abiding word of God;** *for "All flesh is like grass and all its glory like the flower of grass. The grass withers, and the flower falls, but the word of the Lord remains forever." And* **this word is the good news** *that was preached to you.*

There is so much we have to unpack in this passage as it relates to good fruit. First, Peter tells us that we've been born again of imperishable seed, which is the living and abiding word of God. This confirms that 1 John 3 refers to the word of God when it speaks of the "seed" that abides in us. But, the reason Peter uses this language is to re-affirm the fact that our ability to produce good fruit has been restored back to us.

Fruit That Lasts

The spiritual seed of God's word is what activates our ability to produce good fruit for the glory of God. And, then Peter goes on to say that this "word of the Lord" actually remains forever, which means that whatever is produced in our life as a result of that word, will also remain forever.

The nature of God's "seed" is eternal, so whatever is produced from this "seed" will also be eternal. In other words, what is produced by the seed of God's word will last forever.

God intends to bear good fruit in our lives that will remain forever. He desires to produce eternal things that can't be forfeited, lost, or stolen. Jesus confirms this in John 15.

> *John 15:16 - You did not choose me, but I chose you and appointed you* **that you should go and bear fruit and that your fruit should abide**, *so that whatever you ask the Father in my name, he may give it to you.*

God doesn't want good fruit that can be taken away, lost, or forgotten. He doesn't intend to use our lives to produce temporary results, but eternal ones. God wants His people to bear good fruit that stands the test of time and remains when Heaven and Earth pass away.

Chapter 4: Fruit Defined

And, because we're spiritually re-born through God's eternal word, we are now fit for good fruit. What this means is that our old, dead sinful selves were not compatible with the kind of eternal good fruit God wants to bear in our lives. You had to become something entirely new in order to accomplish God's purpose for your life.

This is why it is so important to understand that you have to be re-born as a spiritual child of God in order to produce spiritual, good fruit that lasts forever.

So, when we talk about the fact that God wants His people to bear good fruit, we are talking about spiritual, eternal fruit that results from His spiritual seed, and this fruit is only possible because of our relationship with Him.

But, just like God produces good fruit through His children, the devil tries to copy God. But, the devil can only create a cheap imitation with his own children. As with everything the devil does, he produces a counterfeit of what God does, because he's only capable of less than God. So, the devil and his children have fruit too, but their fruit is evil.

> *Romans 6:21-22 -* **But what fruit were you getting at that time** *from the things of which you are now ashamed? For* **the end of those things is death**. *But now that you have been set free from sin and have become slaves of God, the fruit you get leads to sanctification and its end, eternal life.*

Paul tells us that our old sinful life was producing fruit leading to death. But now, in Christ, we are capable of bearing fruit that leads to more holiness and eternal life. We have to understand that every human being is producing fruit, which is why God specifies that He desires "good" fruit.

Every human being is made in God's image to bear fruit and multiply, which means that every single human is like a tree bearing some kind of fruit; whether good or bad.

And, the fruit you see on a tree, is what determines the kind of tree it is.

For example, if you see apples hanging off a tree, you're not wondering what kind of tree it is. You're looking at an apple tree, because that tree reveals its kind through the fruit it produces. So, the fruit reveals what kind of tree you're looking at.

In fact, Proverbs 1 helps us better understand the fruit of ungodly people.

> *Proverbs 1:29-31 - Because they hated knowledge and did not choose the fear of the Lord, 30 would have none of my counsel and despised all my reproof, 31 therefore* **they shall eat the fruit of their way**, *and have their fill of their own devices.*

Those who hate knowledge, reject the Lord, and don't want His counsel, will eventually eat the kind of fruit that they are planting. And, the author of Proverbs doesn't make that fruit sound good.

Notice how these evil fools reject God, which leads to a kind of fruit they will eat. Their decision to rebel and not fear the Lord is actually symbolic of them planting seeds in their life, and those seeds will eventually produce fruit. And, that fruit will eventually be the kind of life they experience which is the result of their own decisions and actions.

But, contrasted with evil children of the devil, we see children of God bearing fruit in Proverbs 11.

> Proverbs 11:30 - **The fruit of the righteous is a tree of life**, And he who wins souls is wise.

Those who are righteous in God's sight, will produce fruit that not only benefits themselves, but also those around them.

In other words, these righteous individuals are bearing fruit that other people can enjoy, because their good fruit is accessible and visible to everyone in their life.

And, the author says their fruit is a "tree of life" which brings us back to God's original intention for humanity in Genesis. God desired for humanity to eat and enjoy the fruit from the tree of life as they stayed in relationship with their Creator God.

Now, human beings are cut off from that tree of life because of sin. But, Jesus restores us back to a relationship with God, so that now, God offers that same living relationship to others through the fruit He produces in our lives.

Not only does our good fruit benefit other people, but this fruit is a glimpse and invitation into a living relationship with King Jesus. God uses our good fruit to offer eternal life to others. Our good fruit is intended to carry the seed that God will plant in other hearts which will produce the same eternal life we have.

Hopefully you're getting a better idea of the kind of good fruit you were made to produce. Good fruit is what God produces through His children as they make the appropriate preparations for that fruit to be born in their life.

Godly Character = Godly Life

But, you need a clear target to aim for, so I want to give you the clearest possible vision of what God good fruit specifically means. So, my goal throughout the rest of this chapter is to show you everything God means when He says "good fruit."

If you can have a clear definition of God's goal, you'll be more effective in fulfilling God's purpose for your life. And, Paul explains good fruit in Galatians 5.

> *Galatians 5:22-23 - But* **the fruit of the Spirit is** *love, joy, peace, patience, kindness, goodness, faithfulness, gentleness, self-control; against such things there is no law.*

Paul just listed attributes and attitudes and says that this is the fruit of the Spirit. In other words, these attributes result from God's Spirit. This is exactly what we've been talking about.

The Spirit of God intends to produce good fruit in our lives, and this is mainly referring to our character. In other words, God primarily defines good fruit as relating to who we are. This is about imitating the character of Jesus.

Think about it. Love, joy, peace, patience, kindness, goodness, gentleness, faithfulness, and self-control are all perfectly seen

Chapter 4: Fruit Defined

in Jesus. He is the perfect representation and embodiment of these attributes.

So, Paul tells us that a life submitted to God's Spirit, will produce more of these characteristics for people to visibly see and experience. Good fruit is mostly about copying the character of Jesus. This is important to understand as we move forward, because many Christians think God wants them to do a bunch of stuff, while God is actually most concerned about who we are becoming. And, here's why: who we are determines how we live.

When you think about good fruit, think more about how well you imitate the character of Jesus. As you imitate His character, you're producing good fruit for others to enjoy and benefit from.

And, the goal is that this character of Jesus would be planted in others by the power of God's Spirit. But, good fruit isn't only good character and Godly attitudes. There is a lifestyle attached to these attributes, because our lifestyle is determined by who we are. In fact, John the Baptist addressed the importance of a changed life in Matthew 3.

> *Matthew 3:7-10 - But when he saw many of the Pharisees and Sadducees coming to where he was baptizing, he said to them: "You brood of vipers! Who warned you to flee from the coming wrath?* ***Produce fruit in keeping with repentance.*** *And do not think you can say to yourselves, 'We have Abraham as our father.' I tell you that out of these stones God can raise up children for Abraham. The ax is already at the root*

*of the trees, and every tree **that does not produce good fruit** will be cut down and thrown into the fire.*

While John the Baptist is roasting the hypocrites of his day, he makes a powerful statement about a truly transformed life. He tells these hypocrites not to assume God is pleased with them just because they descend from Abraham. John says to bear fruit in keeping with repentance, but what the heck does this mean? He explains in the last sentence, that this refers to producing good fruit. And, for John, this means that they change their life, as proof that they've truly changed their mind about sin and turned to the God of Israel for salvation.

Anyone can claim to be sorry for sin, and anyone can claim to know God, but a transformed life is the real evidence that a person's heart has truly turned from sin to the living God.

So, what is John saying? He's saying that your lifestyle should prove that you belong to God, and this transformed life is what John calls "good fruit." What I find fascinating, is that John says good fruit is the difference between a tree that is thrown into the fire and a tree that isn't.

Why is a tree thrown into the fire? Because it doesn't produce good fruit. And, if people are trees, and this passage refers to eternal judgment, then we can confidently say that true believers who have a transformed lifestyle will avoid eternal judgment. But, those who don't experience a changed lifestyle will be cast into the eternal flame of God's wrath, because their lifestyle proves they haven't truly trusted in Jesus for salvation.

This doesn't mean that we are primarily concerned about behavioral modification. And, this doesn't mean we think good works earn God's salvation, but this does mean that good works reveal a person's salvation. A person who is truly sorrowful over their sin, will live differently by the power of God. And, that transformed life is proof of their genuine faith and repentance.

Quick recap. Good fruit is about who we are and how we live. God desires for us to become more like Jesus but also live more like Jesus as a result. So, when we're bearing good fruit, this means we're imitating Jesus in our thoughts, words, attitudes, desires, interactions, and lifestyle. We should be people that increasingly think more like Jesus, talk more like Jesus, love more like Jesus, respond more like Jesus, and live more like Jesus. This is about growing up into His image and representing Jesus honorably in the earth.

Hebrews 13 and Ephesians 5 both confirm this.

> *Hebrews 13:15 - Through him then let us continually offer up a sacrifice of praise to God, that is,* **the fruit of lips that acknowledge his name**.

The author of Hebrews says that praise to God is the fruit of our lips. The heart overflows through the mouth, so that the words are a reflection of the heart. This is why a heart that belongs to God, will worship and praise God as the "fruit" that is produced through their lips.

> *Ephesians 5:7-11 - Therefore do not become partners with them; for at one time you were darkness, but now you are light in the Lord. Walk as children of light (***for***

the fruit of light is found in all that is good and right and true*), and try to discern what is pleasing to the Lord. Take no part in the **unfruitful works of darkness**, but instead expose them.*

In Ephesians 5, Paul refers to those who are still dead in sin when he tells Christians not to be partners with them in their evil. Instead, Paul tells Christians to walk in the light because they are now light in the Lord. He doesn't tells Christians to live like light in order to become light.

Paul says that someone who is truly a child of light, will produce the spiritual light of Christ through their lives. You don't have to ask the light to shine. The nature of light is that it shines. You don't have to ask the darkness to be dark. That ability is coded into its nature.

It is the same with children of God, who are now the light of Christ. If we are light, there is an appropriate way to live, which is to produce the fruit of light. God expects His children to live a certain way. You don't expect a fish to breathe and live on land. It is made for the water. The ability to live and breathe on land isn't written into its nature. Its nature enables a fish to live under water.

We, as children of God, are made for the light now. It is coded into our nature. And, you'd expect a child of light to live as the light, rather than the darkness.

Paul describes this fruit of light as being good, right, true, and what is pleasing to the Lord. So, good fruit will always honor God, because it will be good, right and true. These are the kind of works we are created for, as children of light. Paul doesn't say we have the light. He says that Christians ARE the light now. Our very nature has been changed, so that spiritual light is naturally produced through our lives.

God Wants Fruit

Remember, good fruit is what God has always wanted. In fact, Jesus tells the unbelieving Jews this exact thing in Matthew 21.

> *Matthew 21:43 - Therefore I tell you, the kingdom of God will be taken away from you and given to* ***a people producing its fruits****.*

Jesus tells the unbelieving Israelites, that God always desired good fruit to be produced through the nation of Israel. God chose Israel to represent Him in the earth, so that the other nations would see the Lord through their way of life.

And, since Israel refused to be loyal to the God of Israel, God is granting His kingdom to those who will produce the fruits He's always desired. This includes believing Jews as well as believing Gentiles.

Jesus says this same kind of thing in one of his parables.

> *Luke 13:6-9 - And he told this parable: "A man had a fig tree planted in his vineyard, and* ***he came seeking fruit*** *on it and found none. 7 And he said to the vinedresser, 'Look, for three years now* ***I have come seeking fruit on this fig tree****, and I find none. Cut it down. Why should it use up the ground?' 8 And he answered him, 'Sir, let it alone this year also, until I*

dig around it and put on manure. **9** Then **if it should bear fruit next year, well and good**; *but if not, you can cut it down.'"*

Notice how Jesus says the owner of the vineyard came looking for fruit. He expected good fruit to be produced, because the primary purpose of having a vineyard is to enjoy its fruit. The owner is looking for what you'd expect from a fig tree: figs. But, he finds none.

The vineyard in this parable is the nation of Israel that didn't give God the good fruit He desired and deserved. Instead, they went and served other gods, and lived in rebellion to God. In this parable, Jesus is the vinedresser who tends to the fig trees, in order to give them chances to bear the good fruit God has always desired. But, they do the opposite, and end up crucifying Jesus on a Roman cross, rather than believing His message.

And, guess what? God does "cut down" the fig tree of Israel, through the Roman Nation in A.D. 70, though they are not completely wiped off the earth. But, God allows destruction to come upon Israel because they refused to give God the good fruit He was worthy of.

I just want you to see the significance of good fruit and how seriously God takes it. God doesn't play around. He desires His people to bear good fruit, multiply His image in the earth and represent Him faithfully.

But, we won't be able to effectively fulfill our God-given purpose without understanding our position in Christ. Our identity and position in Jesus are the foundation that our purpose

Chapter 4: Fruit Defined

is built upon. This concept of identity is absolutely crucial and if we don't understand who we are in Christ, we will not live out the fullest life possible. Period.

Level 2: Position |

Chapter 5: New Identity

After serving in ministry for several years, I've learned that one of the greatest problems plaguing Christians is what we call "identity crisis." Children of God simply don't know who they are. This is usually because they misunderstand the foundation of their identity.

What you have to understand is that our identity in Christ is the foundation of our purpose. What we do, is the result of who we are. So, if we misunderstand who we are in Christ, or why we are in Christ, we will not effectively live out our God-given purpose.

Our identity and purpose are connected. God makes us capable of living out our purpose, by making us a new creation in Christ, because our lifestyle flows from who we are.

So, God doesn't modify our behavior first. He changes the core of who we are so that our lifestyle changes permanently. This doesn't mean God changes our unique personality. This simply means that God changes our spiritual status and identity. God fundamentally changes our standing before Him by declaring us to be something entirely new. God's word shapes reality. So, if God declares something about us, it becomes true by nature of His authoritative word.

And, Paul tells us that those who trust in Jesus for salvation are born again by the Spirit as new creations. They are re-created in Jesus Christ as something completely new. This is good news.

> 2 Corinthians 5:17 - Therefore, **if anyone is in Christ, he is a new creation**. The old has passed away; behold, the new has come.

This passage tells us that we are no longer who we used to be. Our old identity has passed away completely, and it no longer defines us. Our old life no longer has any influence on how God sees us. God doesn't see us according to our sin.

But, this isn't just about how God sees us. This is about who we actually are now. Our old, sinful self is no longer who we are. That old life is gone.

Christians are no longer defined by their sin and darkness, but they're instead, defined by who Jesus is and what He's accomplished for them. Another way to say it is that our works no longer define us because Jesus' death and resurrection now determine our identity.

You might ask why, and, the reason is simple. We are now positioned in Jesus through our faith. We have a newfound relation to Jesus and this new relationship to Christ is what determines who we are.

In other words, our relationship with Jesus forever changes who we are at the core.

God sees us as He sees His own Son. We are now covered in the perfection and righteousness of King Jesus. And, Paul confirms this towards the end of 2 Corinthians 5.

> *2 Corinthians 5:21 - He made Him who knew no sin to be sin on our behalf, so that we might become the righteousness of God in Him.*

Paul says that Christians become the righteousness of God in Jesus. Righteousness refers to right standing before God. We are acceptable and approved before God in Jesus. When we are placed in Jesus through our faith, we become something completely new.

Positioned In Christ

But, what does it mean that we are placed in Jesus? That sounds really weird.

In Exodus, we see Moses ask God to reveal His glory, but God says that Moses can't handle God's glory in his sinful condition. So, God makes a way for Moses to behold His glory by letting Moses see the backside of God's radiant goodness. No sinful human can see God's full glory and live, so God partially reveals His majesty to Moses in a way that he can handle.

But, first, God places Moses in the cleft of a rock so that Moses is tucked away as God's glory passes by. This rock was always an illustration of Jesus. Jesus is the One that we're tucked away in, so that we can behold the glory of the Lord.

Except, unlike Moses in his sinful human condition, Jesus completely re-creates us and covers us in His perfection so that we can stand before God and behold His full glory. And, this will happen fully when we're resurrected to glorified bodies like Jesus.

And, Paul says that we become the righteousness of God through Jesus. There was a divine transaction that took place on the cross where Jesus actually traded places with us. He became our sin, so that we can become His perfection and righteousness. He takes our death so that we can have His life.

So, our new identity is only possible because of Jesus' death and resurrection. Jesus' perfect work on the cross changes who we are, because He made way for us to inherit His standing before the Father.

Jesus has always had a specific kind of relationship with God the Father. He is the perfectly beloved Son of God. And, Jesus actually makes His relationship with the Father accessible to any humans that would trust in Him for salvation. His position before the Father is divinely granted to all who would have faith in His name. Now, that we are in Christ, the Father sees us as He sees His eternally beloved Son. That's insane.

Here's the craziest part. Not only is this newfound identity a completely free gift of God's grace, but this change in identity happens instantly. God doesn't change His view of us over time. The microsecond we believe in Jesus, God completely changes who we are forever. This re-creation happens the moment we choose to believe in Jesus to make us righteous. So, trusting in Jesus means that we believe He will make us acceptable in the sight of God.

Chapter 5: New Identity

I want you to imagine a giant, over-sized coat that God has placed over you. This coat could fit Godzilla, but it rightfully belongs to you even though you don't fit into it. This huge coat represents who you are in Christ, even though your lifestyle doesn't always match up with this identity. This coat represents how God sees you. This identity is still yours and it is forever how God sees you even when you don't live like who you are in Christ.

This giant coat is something you grow up into, which practically means that your lifestyle progressively begins to match up with who your identity is in Jesus. In this sense, you start to fill the coat by living a life that matches up with who you are in God's sight. This is how we make sense of our identity and lifestyle. Though our identity will result in a transformed lifestyle, our lifestyle doesn't determine our identity.

This is good news, because it means that your works and performance don't affect how God sees you. His view of you is not affected by your good or bad works. Now, this isn't an excuse to live in sin, but God does see you through the work of His Son; not your own works.

Even though we inherit Jesus' identity and relationship with the Father, we don't become God as He is. He is uniquely different from us in this regard. But, everything Jesus is, as the perfect human, becomes true of us. We become perfect humans through faith in Him.

And, when we become new, perfect humans through Jesus, this includes a new mind and heart. This new mind and heart results in a transformed life that honors God. Again, your lifestyle is a direct result of who you are.

This means that how you view yourself will affect how you live.

So, I want you to understand that your identity is one of the most important ideas you can understand because it is central to everything in your life. Many of your internal issues are connected to your view of yourself. But, if you can see yourself as God sees you, this will eliminate many of the internal problems you deal with.

Before, we unpack the specifics of our identity, we need to go to John 15 to understand our relation to Jesus now. And, by understanding how we function in relation to Jesus, this will help us live the fullest, most satisfying human life possible.

Just to recap, our new identity is based on who Jesus is and what He's done. These are the only two things that determine who we are now. And, this newfound identity fully belongs to us the very second we believe in Jesus for salvation.

We don't slowly gain more of this identity. God doesn't slowly view us differently over time. It is instantaneous. But, overtime, we will grow up into our new life, and our lifestyle will eventually begin to match up with our identity in Christ.

We Are Branches

Now, let's look at what Jesus says about His followers in John 15. This passage changed my life forever. Once I understood what this passage was really saying, I was able to finally understand how to effectively function as a new creation in Christ.

This chapter in John brought breakthrough in my life, and was a huge answer to prayer. I pray it changes your life too.

John 15:1-4 - **I am the true vine, and my Father is the vinedresser.** *2 Every branch in me that does not bear fruit he takes away, and every branch that does bear fruit he prunes, that it may bear more fruit. 3 Already you are clean because of the word that I have spoken to you. 4 Abide in me, and I in you. As the branch cannot bear fruit by itself, unless it abides in the vine, neither can you, unless you abide in me.*

Before Jesus explains who the disciples are, He explains who He is. If we are to see ourselves correctly, we have to see Jesus rightly. We see ourselves best when we see our Creator clearly.

If you want to better understand who you truly are, you have to see God for who He is. Since our identity is wrapped up in Jesus, it makes sense that we know ourselves better when we know Jesus accurately.

Jesus says that He is the true vine, and The Father is the vinedresser, or the owner of the vineyard. This doesn't mean that Jesus is less than God. This means that Jesus has humbly assumed a role of submission to the Father by taking on human flesh. Then, Jesus says in Verse 2 that His disciples are branches that are connected to Him.

In other words, Jesus' disciples are extensions of Him.

Jesus uses this vine analogy to help His disciples understand that He is the source. He is the one they depend on for life, stability, protection, and provision. Jesus is the reliable foundation, we're built on. He is the unchanging source we are connected to. We draw life from Him. He provides nutrients to us, that we might grow. He is our security and stability in this life. Our connection to Him is our power in life.

By understanding that Jesus is the source, we will see ourselves rightly and function according to our God-given purpose. But, as long as we see ourselves as something we're not, we will function wrongly, and waste our life. You might ask, why? And, it's because we will try and function like something we're actually not. If we're the branches that depend on Jesus, we shouldn't live as anything else, or we'll function improperly.

But, what does it mean that we, as His disciples, are branches? Verse 3 helps us understand. Jesus says that His disciples are already clean through the word of God that they've believed in. This idea of "clean" refers to a branch that is now capable of bearing fruit because it was cleansed and pruned of what made it diseased. This refers to the fact that God has cleansed us of our sins that once prevented us from bearing good fruit.

Not only are we capable of bearing good fruit, but like I've been saying, we are created to bear good fruit. As branches, we depend on Jesus for fruit because He is the vine. This is why He tells His disciples that a branch cannot bear fruit by itself. It is impossible. A branch that is disconnected from the vine, is rendered lifeless and incapable of producing fruit.

So, who are we in Christ? We are branches connected to the vine of Jesus that rely on Him for good fruit to be produced in our lives. Here's a little glimpse into future chapters: as branches, we don't control fruit. We decide how strong our connection is to the vine.

What does this mean practically? It means that we decide how close we are to Jesus, and Jesus controls the fruit that is produced in our lives.

But, I want to make something clear. Part of your identity is that you are eternally secure through your faith in Jesus. In other words, God will never change how He sees you once you're in Christ. Your identity never changes, once you're re-created in Jesus.

God will never change His mind about you, because your identity is based on Jesus, who is eternally the same. He never changes, which means God never changes how He sees you. But, although the Bible makes it clear that you cannot lose your relationship with God, you can definitely forfeit your communion with Him.

What this means is that Christians cannot lose their connection to God, but they can grow distant and disrupt their closeness with God. Sin can disrupt our fellowship with God and decrease our experience of God's presence. We'll talk about this idea later on.

Fighting Spiritual Insecurity

But, what you have to realize is that, one of the biggest dangers for Christians is spiritual insecurity. One of the devil's most powerful tactics is to make a Christian insecure about their faith, and cause them to doubt that they're truly saved.

If we doubt our salvation, we doubt what God declares about us as His children. The devil is an accuser, by nature, and Revelation 12:10 confirms this.

> *Revelation 12:10 - Then I heard a loud voice in heaven, saying, "Now the salvation, and the power, and the kingdom of our God and the authority of His Christ have come,* **for the accuser of our brethren has been thrown down, he who accuses them before our God day and night**.

The devil is referred to as "the accuser" being thrown down. Zechariah 3:1-2 and Job 2:1-6 also speak of the devil and his accusations against God's people.

So, the devil wants to point out our faults. He wants to bring up our failures and remind us of our sin to condemn us and bring shame on believers. He wants to draw us away from God through condemnation and shame that Jesus has already dealt with.

> *Romans 8:1 - There is therefore now* **no condemnation** *for those who are in Christ Jesus.*

If you've trusted in Jesus for salvation, there is literally no more condemnation left for you. Condemnation simply refers to the penalty for our sin. It is about just punishment for sin.

There is not a single ounce of punishment that God has left for us to experience. There is no ounce of shame left for us to endure. Jesus has fully handled every drop of the punishment for our sin, which includes that shame and humiliation that results from being under the penalty of sin.

So, when the devil tries to accuse you, he has no legitimate case, because Jesus is our defense attorney in the court room of Heaven. And, He defends our case perfectly. He's never lost a single court case, because He is perfect justice.

> 1 John 2:1 - *My little children, I am writing these things to you so that you may not sin. But if anyone does sin,* **we have an advocate** *with the Father, Jesus Christ the righteous.*

When the devil accuses us, it is Jesus who stands by our side, defending our case before the Father. Whenever shame or condemnation are trying to penetrate our heart and mind, it is Jesus who stands in front of us to absorb the blow, because He defends us before God the Father.

It's as if the devil and his demons are pointing at us and yelling, "They're guilty! Condemn them! Punish them! They've committed crimes!" Then, Jesus says, "But, they're with me. I've paid their debt." And, God the Father says, "My Son is right. He has covered them and made them acceptable in my sight."

See, God's word about us carries more weight than what anyone else says.

Any time you feel a condemning shame or sense of God's punishment, you're submitting to a false reality. Whenever you think that God is punishing you in some way, you're believing a lie. God will train and discipline His people, and even allow for them to experience the natural consequences of their decisions. But, Jesus has been punished in our place, so we don't have to put ourselves on "time out" when we sin. We don't have to stay distant from God.

This directly relates to our identity, because many Christians experience continual shame that Jesus has fully paid for already. Many believers, including myself, often punish themselves, and live with a sense of condemnation that God is not holding over them. And, this false sense of shame and condemnation is exactly what prevents us from living as children of God.

As long as you're under shame and afraid of Gods's punishment, you can't confidently live as the person He's made you to be.

This is very important to understand. The devil and his demons are destroying the effectiveness of God's children by attacking their identity in Jesus. If the powers of darkness can get us to see ourselves improperly, we'll spend our days living like something God never said we were. So, devil and his demons spend much of their time accusing believers, even when there is no legitimate cause for the accusation.

If we give into his false accusations, we'll end up allowing the powers of darkness to influence how we see ourselves rather than God. 1 John 3:19-20 speaks of this self-condemnation.

> 1 John 3:19-20 - By this we shall know that we are of the truth and reassure our heart before him; 20 **for whenever our heart condemns us, God is greater than our heart**, and he knows everything.

John tells us that our own heart is going to try and condemn us, which means it is expected. Not only will the devil and his demons try and accuse you but so will your own sinful nature.

And, what do we do when the devil, his demons, and our own hearts are trying to speak a deceitful word over us? John tells us that God is greater than our heart, so we submit to God's word about us rather than anyone else's opinion.

Whenever we're tempted to believe something wrong about ourselves, the best way to fight back is to focus on everything God says about us. So, John tells us that we can actually know that we belong to God for certain, which reassures our hearts before Him.

This means that the truth of God's word is what gives our heart confidence to approach Him. But, this also means that God's word is what assures us of who we are in Jesus. We can be secure in our new identity as we grow in knowledge of God's word and trust Him more.

When the enemy comes to distort our view of ourselves, we can choose to pay more attention to what Jesus has done for us, because it is His work and His word that defines us.

But, when the enemy attacks us with a false sense of shame and condemnations he is mainly attacking our salvation. Satan doesn't just want us to doubt who we are in Christ. He wants us to doubt that our salvation is secure in Christ forever. He wants us to believe that we can lose our position in Jesus.

If the devil can get us to believe that we can lose God's free gift of grace and salvation, then we'll believe that our self-worth is based on our obedience.

Christians think they can lose their relationship with God, and this causes them to live with a low sense of confidence and assurance. They wake up each day just trying to not go to hell, instead of enjoying God and aiming to honor Him with their lives. This makes God's people ineffective, because they spend their lives trying to prove their salvation rather than serving God out of love and assurance.

Listen, if you're in Christ, you're locked in that position forevermore because you've made the decision to commit your loyalty to King Jesus. And, Jesus responds to your faith by sealing you forever with His Spirit for the day of redemption.

> *Ephesians 1:13-14 - In him you also, when you heard the word of truth, the gospel of your salvation, and believed in him,* **were sealed with the promised Holy Spirit***, 14 who is the guarantee of our inheritance until we acquire possession of it, to the praise of his glory.*

> *Ephesians 4:30 - And do not grieve the Holy Spirit of God,* **by whom you were sealed for the day of redemption***.*

These two passages of Scripture teach us that we are sealed and marked by God's Spirit. His Spirit is a guarantee of our inheritance in Heaven. God stamps us with His mark of approval, and that mark is his eternal presence within us.

Paul specifically says that we're sealed with God's Spirit for the day of redemption when we will be glorified with Jesus. That day is guaranteed for anyone filled with God's Spirit. That Heavenly inheritance is promised for anyone filled with God's Spirit.

These promises and guarantees wouldn't be true if someone could lose their salvation and forfeit the Spirit of God within them.

This is important for you to understand. The foundation of your Christian life is security and assurance. So, if you rob a Christian of their assurance of salvation, you rob them of their effectiveness as believers.

We can only serve God well, when we know our soul is eternally secure in God's hands. But, once we doubt whether or not we're going to Heaven, we begin to spend our time trying to make sure we're saved rather than advancing God's Kingdom.

So, let me assure you that the Bible teaches the eternal security of a Christian, which means that you cannot lose your salvation or relationship with God. But, Paul does tell us to examine ourselves to see whether we're in the faith. There are signs that you have true saving faith. A true Christian will have proof that they really belong to God.

> *2 Corinthians 13:5 -* **Examine yourselves, to see whether you are in the faith**. *Test yourselves. Or do you not realize this about yourselves, that Jesus Christ is in you?—unless indeed you fail to meet the test!*

Paul tells us to examine our lives to see if there is reason to believe we belong to Jesus. But, once you test your life and see evidence of real faith, you no longer have to spend your time trying to make sure you're truly saved.

If you're proven to be a legitimate child of God, you can be certain that God will not change HIs mind about you. God's view of you was never based on your works. God's view of you is based on His Son's work on the cross.

In, fact the author of Hebrews, tells us that Jesus is unchanging. He is eternally the same.

> *Hebrews 13:8 - Jesus Christ is the same yesterday and today and forever.*

Jesus is eternally consistent and forever the same. He is not subject to change. God is who He's always been and who He will be forevermore. This makes God completely reliable and trustworthy. And, this also means that God's view of us never changes, since He sees us through the perfection of His Son. Right? His view of us is based on the unchanging Son.

Think about it for a minute. Your identity and position in Christ are not subject to change, because Jesus is not subject to change. If He's unchanging, and our identity is based on Him, then our standing with God never changes. He never changes His view of us, because He sees us as He sees His own eternally beloved Son, Jesus. God has graciously decided to love us forevermore as His own children. And, His love becomes the only defining factor in our life.

In other words, God's love for us has to be the main thing we identify with. Our identity and self-worth are wrapped up in one thing, and that is the love of God. This is why John the Apostle would consistently refer to himself as "the one whom Jesus loved." John didn't allow anything to determine his value and identity except the love of God.

Chapter 5: New Identity

If you were to ask John who he was, he would answer, "I am loved by God." At the core of John's identity and value was one central thing: God's steadfast love. God's love is the only thing that defines us forevermore. And, that love has been demonstrated through Jesus' death and resurrection.

We also have to understand that God's love for us is not because of us, but in spite of us. And, that might sound offensive at first, but it is actually quite liberating. God doesn't love us for any reason except that He is gracious. We inherently do not deserve the love of God, so His decision to love us was not because of anything we could give or do.

God's love towards us has nothing to do with our performance. Our failures or successes don't affect His love for us. The love of God is in spite of our failures and not because of our accomplishments. This is the good news of His faithful love.

And, that love of God becomes the source of our identity and value. God's love is the only thing that I allow to define me. This is what it means to have true identity. It means when you look in the mirror, you see a child of God who is loved by the Father. Your greatest position and title in this life is "child of God."

And, God promises that as His child, you cannot be separated from this divine love that He's poured out onto you.

> *Romans 8:38-39 - For I am sure that neither death nor life, nor angels nor rulers, nor things present nor things to come, nor powers, nor height nor depth, nor*

*anything else in all creation, will be able to **separate us from the love of God in Christ Jesus our Lord**.*

We cannot be separated from the love of God which defines us forevermore. But, this assurance and security should not motivate us to live in sin.

In fact, this amazing truth should result in a transformed life. In light of our eternal security and assurance, there is an appropriate and reasonable life that you would expect. In the next chapter, we'll talk about this transformed life more in detail.

Level 2: Position |
Chapter 6: Transformed Life

Recently, I preached 2 Corinthians 5 to my youth group, and I thought it was a powerful moment for our little community. One of the main things I told them was that they should be less concerned about how they are perceived, and more concerned about how they're living.

I told them not to focus on merely appearing to be a Christian, but instead to focus on actually being a Christian. I wanted them to learn to live as children of God instead of needing to prove to everyone they were children of God.

In my own life, there have been times where I was more concerned about how others perceive me. I was focused more on how I appeared. I wanted so badly to be thought of as a Christian. And, we should be concerned about shining our light and representing Jesus well, but my reasoning was wrong. I had a wrong order of priorities.

I discovered that any "good things" I was doing for God, was just to re-affirm myself, rather than to honor God. I was more concerned about proving I was a Christian when I should've been more concerned with honoring God because He's worthy.

And, I think many believers can relate to this. You might be someone who does a lot of good things for God, but you only "feel" saved and loved by God when you're living the right way.

But, should we only live for God in order to feel loved and approved by Him? Should we only obey God to prove the genuineness of our faith? Should we only serve God to re-affirm our salvation? Should we love God to feel more secure about who we are in Christ?

I don't think so. When I read Scripture, it seems more like we should honor, serve and obey God because we love Him from a place of security and assurance. In other words, our good works are in response to God's love and not the cause of His love.

Prove It With Fruit

So, what does this mean for our good works and holy living?

It has taken me years to finally understand this: what we do is a result of who we are. Many Christians get this backwards. Good thing we've already established in the last chapter that God changes who we are, so that our lifestyle changes as a natural result.

Don't get me wrong. God wants to change your life, but without a changed heart and a new identity, any behavioral change would only be temporary, or spiritually unhelpful. In Matthew 7, Jesus addresses this idea of works and He refers to our lifestyle as "fruit." Sound familiar?

Chapter 6: Transformed Life

> *Matthew 7:15-20 - Beware of false prophets, who come to you in sheep's clothing but inwardly are ravenous wolves. 16 You will **recognize them by their fruits**. Are grapes gathered from thornbushes, or figs from thistles? 17 So, every healthy tree bears good fruit, but the diseased tree bears bad fruit. 18 A healthy tree cannot bear bad fruit, nor can a diseased tree bear good fruit. 19 Every tree that does not bear good fruit is cut down and thrown into the fire. 20 Thus **you will recognize them by their fruits**.*

Jesus says that you will recognize a person by the fruit they produce in their life. He says that a good tree won't produce bad fruit and a bad tree won't produce good fruit. Why will a certain kind of tree only produce a certain kind of fruit? Because a tree can't produce what is contrary to its nature. The nature of the tree is wired by God to produce a certain kind of fruit.

This means that an evil person will not have a lifestyle that produces good fruit, while a child of God will not have a lifestyle that produces bad fruit. And, I intentionally use the word "lifestyle" because Jesus is not talking about a moment of good or bad fruit, but a lifetime of good or bad fruit. This is referring to the consistent fruit that is produced longterm over the course of someone's life.

The main point in this is that a true, born-again Christian will not live in sin and spiritual darkness as their consistent way of life. Instead, a Christian will aim to live a life of holiness in the light of Christ. This is exactly what 1 John teaches us.

> 1 John 1:6-7 - **If we say we have fellowship with him while we walk in darkness**, we lie and do not practice the truth. 7 But **if we walk in the light, as he is in the light**, we have fellowship with one another, and the blood of Jesus his Son cleanses us from all sin.

A genuine child of God will not live in the spiritual darkness. Sin will not be their habitual way of life, because it is contrary to their new nature in Christ. Instead, they will live in the light, though they may stumble into the darkness at times. This isn't about perfection. This is about resting in Jesus' perfection, and living a new life that results from faith and assurance.

> 1 John 3:9-10 - **No one born of God makes a practice of sinning**, for God's seed abides in him; and **he cannot keep on sinning**, because he has been born of God. 10 By this it is evident who are the children of God, and who are the children of the devil: whoever does not practice righteousness is not of God, nor is the one who does not love his brother.

John also says love will be the central focus of our new life. A life that honors God is a life that is full of love for God and people. True children of God will aim to live a holy life that is full of love, not to earn salvation, but because they're saved.

And, John also makes it clear that the "seed" that dwells in believers is what keeps them from living in sin. Good thing we've already discussed that this seed is the Spirit of God. Remember, His presence makes us new creations.

Our new nature is connected to our new life of obedience to God. This goes back to the idea that a Christian is not

Chapter 6: Transformed Life

someone who has to fake fruit or force it by their own efforts and strength. A Christian is someone who's nature has been changed by God so they're now capable of living a life that honors God. I know I've been saying it repeatedly, but I want you to get it. A new identity comes before a transformed lifestyle.

So, we have to see our good works as the proof of our salvation and not the reason for our salvation. In other words, our good works don't earn us right standing with God. Instead, these good works are proof of our right standing with God.

Remember, we are children of God through our faith in Jesus. But, how do you know you actually have real, saving faith? Faith is invisible. There has to be evidence of an invisible faith. And, James speaks of this in his letter.

> *James 2:17 - So also* **faith by itself, if it does not have works**, *is dead.*

> *James 2:26 - For as the body apart from the spirit is dead, so also* **faith apart from works is dead**.

One of the signs that you have true saving faith in Jesus, is that your life produces good works. And, good works refers to your words, actions, and attitudes towards people.

But, I've seen Christians take this truth the wrong way. Instead, of resting in Jesus as their reason for confidence, they begin to trust in their works for confidence alongside Jesus.

Our Reason For Confidence

What we have to understand is that Jesus is our confidence before God, not our good works.

However, our good works show us that we have real faith in Jesus. Think of it like this. Jesus is the only reason someone is given eternal life. But, if you claim to know Jesus, yet see no evidence of true saving faith, do you have reason to feel confident?

The answer is no. You have to be certain you know Him by having evidence, and that evidence will come through a transformed life. But, here's the tension for believers. Though, our good works matter as evidence of our faith, we shouldn't spend our lives obsessing over our good works as if that is the main priority.

Here's what I mean. Once we see evidence of God's Spirit dwelling within us, we no longer have to spend our life looking for proof that we truly know Jesus. This doesn't mean that once we see enough clear evidence of saving faith that we now have permission to live however we want.

In fact, true saving faith isn't just a moment of belief but a lifetime of continual believing loyalty to King Jesus.

Yes, good works prove our faith, but some people will distort this idea and spend their entire life trying to make sure they're really a child of God by doing enough good works. But, again, the reason for our eternal security is Jesus.

Chapter 6: Transformed Life

The evidence that we know Him is that God produces good works through us over the course of our lifetime. Faith is simply taking God at His word and trusting Him to get us into His Kingdom rather than trusting in our good works.

I've seen two unhealthy extremes within the Christian world. Some people say good works don't matter at all, because we are saved through faith alone. Then, some Christians give too much weight to their good works and emphasize their obedience over Jesus' work on the cross.

And, we as Christians need to be people that are more focused on what Jesus has done for us rather than what we're doing for Him.

Living holy and producing good fruit should never make you feel more saved or secure. In the same way, falling into sin and darkness at certain moments shouldn't cause you to feel less saved and less secure in Christ. But, there is a biblical balance to maintain.

There have been times where I view God's grace as an excuse to sin, when His grace is actually reason to live free from sin. Then, there are times where I choose to obey God, but I'm more proud of my good works than I am about knowing Jesus who saved me.

So, ask yourself, are you more proud of what you do for God or what He's done for you? This doesn't mean that you cannot have any sense of pride in what God accomplishes through your life. This just means that we need to see our good works in view of Jesus' ultimate work.

God is honored by our obedience, but He is not impressed. Anything good that we do for God is only possible because of what Christ has first done for us. And, this awareness is what keeps us humble as we serve God, but it also helps us view our good works as God does. Jesus gets all the credit and glory for anything good that comes through our life, but we are the vessels that He chooses to use.

As children of God, our works matter to God, but we have to know what this really means. John 15 should help us understand this even more.

> *John 15:4-5 - Abide in me, and I in you.* **As the branch cannot bear fruit by itself, unless it abides in the vine, neither can you, unless you abide in me.** *5 I am the vine; you are the branches. Whoever abides in me and I in him, he it is that bears much fruit,* **for apart from me you can do nothing**.

Jesus says that we are the branches that are connected to Him. This means that our good fruit is related to our position in Jesus. Good fruit is produced in our life because of our closeness to Jesus.

So, when we see obedience, good works, and spiritual service happening in our life, who is really the source of these things? To answer this, we have to look at Jesus' last statement. Jesus says, "apart from me you can do nothing."

Without Jesus, would we be able to produce good fruit? Nope. Good fruit is only possible because of Jesus, who enables us to be fruitful. This doesn't mean that unbelievers can't accomplish anything. It just means that any "good" things they accomplish in this life have no eternal significance for them. They might be "good" deeds but they have no eternal value.

We can only be fruitful branches because we are connected to God through Jesus. So, our good works are the direct result of being connected to God. It is a natural consequence.

As believers, God doesn't ask us to do anything that He won't enable us to do. His own divine power and grace is what works through us to produce obedience, service and love. This was a revelation for me, because I spent much of my life thinking that I was the source and ultimate cause of my own good works.

While we do have a responsibility in the fruit-production process, we are not the ultimate cause of that good fruit. We do have the free will to obey, love and serve, but it is God who works through our own freewill decisions to produce good fruit.

So, God isn't forcing us to obey and serve Him. We exercise free will to love God and do these things ourselves, but it is God's power and grace that enables us to effectively accomplish these good works.

I'll explain this more in-depth in future chapters, but for now, I just want you to see good works the way God does, and how your identity relates to your productivity.

Level 2: Position |
Chapter 7: Heavenly Attributes

Your view of yourself will determine how effec-tive and fruitful your life is. No one ever told me this growing up. I focused so much on the external behavioral modification, and never spent time letting God show me who I was.

Now I see myself much clearer, because I've chosen to let God tell me who I am. And, if I had a right view of myself growing up, this would've prevented so many problems. I would've been way more effective for the Kingdom of God.

Most of my life, I lived with a wrong view of myself because I let other people (including myself) tell me who I was, or who I was supposed to be. This identity crisis left me crippled in more ways than one. Instead of living out God's purpose for my life, I spent most of my life insecure and afraid. I spent my life wondering what everyone was thinking about me, and even believing assumptions I had about what they were thinking.

One of my greatest fears was public speaking. I still have the temptation to be afraid of public speaking and large crowds, but I don't give into that fear the way I used to. But, now I know how to resist it, because I know who God has made

Chapter 7: Heavenly Attributes

me to be. And, this crippling fear continued until I was 21 years old.

In school, I could barely say my name in front of the classroom without anxiety hitting me like a freight train. And, when it was time for project presentations, I would have rather died than stand up in front of all my classmates. Instead of talking, I'd spend my time drawing thought bubbles above everyone's head as if I knew what they were thinking about me.

It was a terrifying thing to talk in front of crowds. And, now I know it was because I didn't know who I was. This caused me to live insecure and deathly afraid of people's opinions. This is what the Bible calls "fear of man" and it was a snare for my life. This was the story of my life for many years.

Eventually, I grew close to God, matured in my faith, and as a result, I realized that God had gifted me to teach and preach His word. Isn't that ironic? The very thing I was deathly afraid of, is exactly what God created me to do. And, sometimes I wonder if the devil and his demons knew this. But, now I stand in front of crowds to teach and preach God's word, and I know this is what He designed me for.

God has gifted me to preach His word, and I only know this now because I have spent enough time in God's presence to discover it.

What I mean is that I have come to know God better over the years. I've grown closer to Him, through seeking Him in prayer and His word, and as a result, I've come to see myself clearer. By knowing God better, He has organically led me by His Spirit into my God-given purpose.

This happened over time, though, and I wasn't necessarily on an intentional journey to discover my gifts or purpose. I just wanted to know God better and be as close to Him as possible. And, as I pursued Jesus, He led me into my purpose and helped me discover who I am.

God showed me things I wasn't even looking for. But, I would've never started walking out my God-given purpose without first seeing myself as God does.

If there's one thing I want you to really hear, it's this: you see yourself best when you know your Creator better. And, let me tell you, it is the most amazing thing to see yourself how God see you. However, it starts with knowing Him in His word, in prayer, and many other ways, and then, over time God begins to give you His heart for others and yourself.

In this chapter, we're going to explore the specific details of who we are in Jesus. I don't just want to explain the nature of your identity. I want you to see every detail possible. And, the better you see yourself in light of God, the clearer God's path and purpose for your life will become. We're going to unpack the key characteristics of your identity in Jesus.

Every characteristic of your identity that we're going to unpack, will have more implications for your life than you know.

So, if I can encourage you, I would say to really pray through these attributes with God and meditate on them. Think through them and consider what this means for your life. I want you to think about how these characteristics should change your way of life and your view of the world.

Chapter 7: Heavenly Attributes

I don't just want these facts to hit your brain. I want this truth to transform your life. And, that means that you will have to process these truths in God's presence through prayer.

I am not going to give you an exhaustive list of everything that you are in Christ. Instead, I want to focus on those attributes that will be the most helpful for your life.

I'm not saying the other attributes don't matter. But, an entire book could be written just on our identity in Christ, so I am only going to highlight those aspects that Paul emphasizes in Ephesians 1.

As we go through these different characteristics, I want you to understand two key things. Who we are is the direct result of what God does to us. How God treats us changes who we are. And, secondly, these traits are inherited from Jesus, who embodied these first. These two ideas are very important to keep in mind as we move forward.

Blessed In Christ

First, let's look at Ephesians 1:3 where we see, arguably, the most important aspect of our identity in Christ. We are blessed because God blesses us.

> *Ephesians 1:3 - Blessed be the God and Father of our Lord Jesus Christ,* **who has blessed us** *in Christ with every spiritual blessing in the heavenly places,*

This has been one of the most impactful verses in my life. Once the Lord showed me what this verse was really saying, everything changed for me. Paul breaks out in praise because of all the Lord has done for us in Christ. He begins blessing God for blessing us in Jesus.

Paul says that we are blessed in Christ, and everything else about our identity relates to this idea of being blessed. Paul is going to list all of our blessings and benefits that we have in Jesus, but first, he declares that we have been blessed by God.

What does it mean to be blessed? If we don't define "blessing" the way God does, we'll miss out on this profound truth.

Paul says we have every "spiritual blessing," which means he's not speaking of temporary, earthly benefits like money, success, fame, physical health, physical safety, or material possessions. This doesn't mean God won't bless us with these things at times, but Paul is speaking primarily of the invisible, immaterial blessings that are hidden in Christ.

We have access to all of the spiritual riches of Christ. Remember, when Jesus triumphed on the cross, He gained back all of the spiritual riches that Adam and Eve forfeited through their sin.

Jesus then grants us access to all of these spiritual blessings. He shares His inheritance with us. So, when Paul says that we are blessed, he's talking about an inward condition, rather than a state of external circumstances. Since God has blessed us, we are now blessed. It is who we are. As a Christian, part of your identity is that you are eternally, completely blessed in Jesus.

And, the best part is that we have been blessed to the fullest possible extent. Paul says that God blesses us with every spiritual blessing. He doesn't hold anything back. As children of God, we are given instant access to all the spiritual blessings and riches of Jesus.

You cannot be more blessed than you are right now in Christ. We are declared fully blessed the microsecond that we believe in Jesus Christ for salvation. In Christ, God has brought us to the highest point of human existence. We cannot climb any higher than where God has brought us to. We are spiritually rich and blessed in the fullest sense.

I want you to understand that regardless of your worldly circumstances, you are blessed to the fullest extent in Christ Jesus. This is your reality, whether you feel it or not. So, you cannot be more blessed, no matter what you gain or achieve in this life. Nothing in this life makes you anymore blessed, because these are spiritual blessings in the heavenly places that are based on Jesus.

This also means that nothing in this life can make you less blessed because you are fully blessed forevermore, regardless of your life circumstances.

> This is why in *Psalm 23, David can say "The Lord is my Shepherd*, **I shall not want**." As children of God, we literally lack nothing. We are not in want of anything, because Jesus blessed us enough to be constantly content in Him.

You might argue that we still lack progress, spiritual growth, and maturity in Christ. But, these things refer to your lifestyle here on earth and not your eternal position in Jesus. You are still perfect and holy in the sight of God.

So, in one sense you lack nothing because you're perfect in the sight of God. But, in another sense you need to grow up into the image of Christ while you're here on earth.

I don't want you to think that contentment means complacency. Contentment is a state of mind and condition of our hearts. Complacency means that we are no longer making progress, because we've become inactive and lazy. And, that's not what God desires for you. Make sure that your contentment doesn't turn into complacency and laziness.

I'm just trying to show you that you have reason for complete satisfaction and contentment. Jesus has fulfilled us completely. He has satisfied our soul forever. This is why Jesus refers to Himself as the bread of life and the living water, because He completely satisfies the hunger and thirst of our soul. We are completely blessed forevermore.

And, remember that this is ultimate reality regardless of how our life looks, because this condition is based on Jesus and His work on the cross. No one and nothing can make you more or less blessed.

Notice, how Paul says God "has" blessed us in Christ, which means this is a past-tense action that God has already completed. The microsecond we trusted in Christ for salvation, we were blessed with every possible spiritual blessing in Jesus.

But, I'm sure you're confused right now. You read about all the blessings in Scripture, but then you look at your life, and there's a problem. There are many blessings in Scripture that you aren't seeing in your life. So, how are you completely

Chapter 7: Heavenly Attributes

blessed, when there are tons of blessings that you aren't experiencing in your life? The answer is actually quite simple.

God gives us ACCESS to every spiritual blessing at the moment we trust in Jesus, but the EXPERIENCE of those blessings increases as we grow up in our relationship with Jesus. Having access to something isn't the same as enjoying and experiencing that thing.

Imagine you've never had a smart phone. Some of you don't have to imagine because you've genuinely never owned a smart phone. But, let's imagine that someone just bought you the newest iPhone, with all of the newest features. This phone will make your life easier in so many ways because of all the different functions it has. You've been blessed by someone.

But, instead of opening the box and using the phone, you leave it in the box and place it neatly on your shelf. There are so many different benefits available to you on that phone, but you're not using it, so it does you no good. After several months, you finally unbox the phone and turn that thing on.

You go through the setup process and start using it, and as you do, you start discovering all of the helpful capabilities on that phone. It makes your life easier in so many ways.

Before you unboxed it and started using it, that iPhone didn't benefit you. It was available to you, but you had to do something in order to experience the benefits of that phone. You had a responsibility to unbox it, turn it on, go through the setup process, and learn how to use it.

This is what many Christians don't understand about all of their blessings in Christ. God has given them countless gifts, but those gifts are sitting on the shelf of their life collecting dust. You might want to write this down: being blessed is not the same as living blessed. That might sound weird at first, but Peter explains this idea in his second letter to the church.

> 2 Peter 1:2-3 - **May grace and peace be multiplied to you in the knowledge of God** and of Jesus our Lord. 3 His divine power has granted to us **all things that pertain to life and godliness, through the knowledge of him** who called us to his own glory and excellence.

Peter says that grace and peace are multiplied to us in the knowledge of God. Grace and peace are the spiritual blessings that we have available in Christ. But, Peter says those blessings are accessed through the knowledge of God, which is found in His word.

In other words, God has a specific system in place to deliver to His people what they need. These blessings might be available to us, but there is a way that we experience them.

Peter goes on to say that everything we need to live a Godly life is found in the knowledge of God. This means that every spiritual blessing God knows you need, is actually experienced through a growing knowledge of God in His word.

This means that as you read the Bible to know God better, you will begin to experience all of the spiritual blessings in Christ that have your name on it.

You might be fully blessed in Christ, with access to all of His spiritual riches, but if you aren't doing your part to walk in the enjoyment of these blessings, what good is it? You can enter into Heaven completely blessed, without having lived in the fullness of God's blessings.

Just know that part of your God-given identity in Christ includes being completely blessed for all eternity. You are blessed in Christ, and nothing can change that. You lack nothing in Him. You don't need anything more, you just need to see what you already have in Christ.

Chosen For A Purpose

A second element of our God-given identity is found in the first part of Ephesians 1:4.

> Ephesians 1:4 - even as he chose us in him before the foundation of the world, that we should **be holy and blameless before him**.

This verse declares that children of God are chosen by God. This is one of the blessings that Christ extends to us. God chooses us, which makes us chosen. And, Jesus is the true chosen one. He is the elect one of God that succeeds where Israel (God's chosen nation) failed.

> 1 Peter 2:6 - For it stands in Scripture: "Behold, I am laying in Zion a stone, a cornerstone **chosen and precious**, and whoever believes in him will not be put to shame."

> *Luke 23:35 - 35 And the people stood by, watching, but the rulers scoffed at him, saying, "He saved others; let him save himself, if he is the Christ of God, **his Chosen One!**"*

In these two passages, we see that Jesus is the chosen one of God the Father. He is the original elect, and this is important for us to understand. We are only able to be the elect, or "chosen" people of God, because Jesus shares His unique position with us. We inherit this trait of being the chosen of God, through our faith in Jesus, who is the true chosen one.

Now, I don't want to get into some weird debate about the logistics of God choosing us, because that is a book all by itself. I do want to say that no matter what theological lens you bring to this verse, God has selected us to be His children. We have been hand-selected out of the billions of people that have ever walked this planet.

When God is deciding who He will choose to become His beloved children, He points His finger at you. When God is deciding who will inherit His eternal kingdom with Jesus, He calls you out of the crowds by name.

I don't know if you've ever been selected for something really significant, but there's an unexplainable feeling that comes from being chosen by someone important or for something important.

But, being chosen in and of itself isn't always amazing. Have you ever been chosen for something that wasn't great? Maybe you were chosen by someone you didn't really like? I

Chapter 7: Heavenly Attributes

can definitely say yes to both. Obviously, just being selected isn't enough cause for excitement.

What really matters is who is choosing you and what you are being chosen for. This help us understand the immense weight and significance of being chosen by God.

Let's frame up God correctly before we unpack this.

The Lord God of Israel is the only true God. He is three in one. He is the Creator of everything that exists in both the physical and spiritual realm. He invented time, space and matter. He is endless. He is eternal, which means has no beginning or end. He always has been, and He always will be. He possesses all possible power, authority, and rule. He is the supreme being in charge. He is sovereignly ruling and in complete control. He creates everything by speaking it into existence and He holds everything together by that same powerful word.

He is self-sufficient, which means He relies on nothing outside of Himself. He is perfect righteousness and pure holiness. His radiant goodness and majesty causes angels to cover themselves as they declare His praise. He dwells in unapproachable light because He is so uniquely set apart and holy. He has no equal. He is unrivaled and unmatched. He is the unstoppable God who dispenses perfect justice as the Almighty Judge of all things.

That amazing God has hand-picked you out of billions of people to be in His divine family. That God has selected you by name to become His beloved child. Now, do you see the significance of being chosen by God? At the core of who you are, you are someone who is chosen by God because He loves you. This is your identity forevermore.

God is the only one who's opinion matters. Think about it. When every person is standing before God's throne on the day of judgment, who's opinion will be the only one that matters?

You won't be thinking about anyone else's opinion. You won't be thinking about who wanted you or rejected you during your life on earth. The only thing you'll care about is God's opinion and verdict about you. And, this Almighty Judge has made His decision about you. He has made an eternal decree to choose you as His own beloved child. Isn't that enough?

Why would we ever care about anyone else's approval when God Almighty has told you that He has chosen you? His opinion outweighs anyone else's. Any rejection or acceptance we experience from people is overshadowed by God's decision to choose us.

Holy And Blameless

What exactly does God choose us for? There has to be a reason for God's choice. And, God makes clear why He chooses us. He chose us to be holy and blameless before Him in love.

This is the next dimension of our identity in Christ. Paul says that God has chosen us in Christ to be holy and blameless before Him in love. This word "holy" means set apart from the rest. When something or someone is holy, they are sacred and set apart by God and for God. But, Paul adds

Chapter 7: Heavenly Attributes

in "blameless" just to clarify that "holy" also means perfect and spotless. It refers to moral perfection, which means the blameless person can't be accused or penalized for sin.

So, if God chose us for the purpose of being holy and blameless, does this happen immediately or later on in Heaven? And, the answer is both. This has two dimensions to it.

In Christ, you were made holy and blameless the microsecond you trusted in Jesus for salvation. God granted you the holiness and perfection of His own Son, so that in Christ, we perfectly fulfill the Law through His perfect life.

Jesus covers us in His righteousness and perfection, which sets us apart from the unbelieving world. We are made holy and blameless as Jesus, which makes us set apart for God's glory and His good purpose.

But, let's be honest. We don't live morally perfect and upright. We struggle with sin because of our sinful nature. So, yes God chose us to be made instantly blameless, spotless and holy through our faith in Jesus. That is our standing before God. This is who we are at the core.

But, we don't always live like who we truly are in Christ. We are growing into the image of Christ and living more like Him each day. This is a process. There are two dimensions to this idea of holiness. One dimension is our eternal position, which we call "justification," and the other one is our process of transformation which we call "sanctification."

We were chosen by God to instantly become holy and blameless through our faith, but also to live holy and blameless. This means that we will spend the rest of our life matching up our lifestyle with who we truly are in Jesus. As we are transformed by God's grace, our lifestyle will begin to match the identity we have in Jesus. But, we have to remember that God always sees us as perfect and holy because of our faith in Jesus.

This is good news. It means that God doesn't see us any differently as we're progressing in our faith. His view of us doesn't changed based on our performance. We are a finished product in the sight of God, but as long as we are in this fleshly body, we have progress to make.

Our entire life, we will be progressing towards Jesus, until one day, when God removes our sinful nature by resurrecting us to a new glorified body. And, that new glorified body will perfectly fit who we are right now in Jesus. It will be a perfect match.

On that final day, we will be revealed as what we've always been in Christ. But, right now our sinful, human bodies aren't compatible with our spiritual identity in Jesus. The two are at odds. This is how Paul describes the war between the Spirit and the flesh.

Just remember, our position and identity in the sight of God, don't change. On that great day, our glorified bodies will reveal the full glory of what these current, sinful bodies have concealed. God sees us as holy and blameless now, but on that great day, everyone will see us fully as holy, blameless, children of God.

Divine Inheritance

You are uniquely set apart to God as perfect, blameless, righteous children of God, all because of Jesus. And, this leads us perfectly to the next characteristic of our identity.

We are children of God, that have been lovingly adopted into God's divine family. God treats us as His own beloved Son, so that we are now His beloved children.

> *Ephesians 1:5 - he predestined us* **for adoption to himself as sons** *through Jesus Christ, according to the purpose of his will,*

We have been adopted into God's divine family, and this adoption is one of the main blessings that Paul is praising God for in Ephesians 1. We used to be orphans, living on the streets. We were oppressed and mastered by the devil and sin.

But, Jesus set us free from our old masters in order to belong to God as our loving Father. He rescued us and brought us into His own home where we are treated as His own. That's crazy.

Paul says that God predestined us for adoption, which means God always intended to adopt those who would trust in His beloved Son for salvation. This is how God chooses to treat someone who has faith in Christ. God wipes us off, makes us new, and invites us into His eternal family where we find our belonging and acceptance.

Paul takes this idea even further in Romans 8.

*Romans 8:16-17 - The Spirit himself bears witness with our spirit that **we are children of God, 17 and if children, then heirs—heirs of God and fellow heirs with Christ,** provided we suffer with him in order that we may also be glorified with him.*

According to this passage, children of God are co-heirs with Christ that get to inherit everything the Father makes available to His children.

Hold on. You're telling me that God grants us access to the full inheritance of Jesus Christ? Yes, this is exactly what Paul wants us to understand.

As children of God, we find belonging and acceptance forevermore as beloved children. We are apart of God's divine family where we have perfect love and care from our Heavenly Father. God takes it a step further, though.

Paul tells us that everything Jesus has gained through His death and resurrection, actually has our name on it. Jesus shares His entire inheritance and riches with us so that they now rightfully belong to us. This doesn't mean we deserve His inheritance. It just means that we have been granted the inheritance of Jesus.

Picture this. You're an orphan and you've only known the darkness of the streets. You've only known the oppression of the devil and sin. One day you encounter this incredibly rich, honorable man named Jesus, and He invites you to His Father's mansion.

As you're approaching this mansion, you realize that you don't belong here. This place is too good for you. But, this Jesus reassures you that you're welcome here. He brings you into His mansion, where you meet His Father. And, before you can say anything, His Father tells you that He wants to adopt you into His family. You're stunned. You're not good enough for this kind of a life and family.

The Father reassures you that He is serious. Everything inside of you wants to accept this gracious offer, so you accept. He then tells you that He has something to show you.

You follow Him through every room of the mansion where you see what seems like endless riches and possessions. He then takes you to the top floor, where He points to His vast land. His land goes farther than your eye can see. You realize that this is no ordinary rich family.

He tells you that everything He owns, His Son will inherit. Then, He looks straight at you and tells you that He's decided to write your name in the will so that you get to inherit everything His Son will. You just became a co-heir with Jesus, so that all of His riches, reputation, position, and possessions become your own. He holds nothing back from you.

You're speechless. This all happened in a matter of moments. You went from living in oppression and darkness to inheriting everything this man Jesus has.

This is exactly what took place the microsecond you trusted in Jesus for salvation. In fact, God has done way more than any one parable could fully capture. Our imagination cannot come up with a scenario that fully communicates what God has done for us in adopting us.

> Hebrews 1:2 - But in these last days he has spoken to us by his Son, whom **he appointed the heir of all things**, through whom also he created the world.

Jesus is said to be the appointed heir of all things, and rightfully so. He is the One through whom all things exist, and He is the purpose of all things. So, Jesus is the origin of all things, He sustains all things, and He is the ultimate reason for all things. Think about what this includes. Jesus definitely has every right to own everything that exists since He created it all.

This inheritance of Christ has our names on it not because we deserve it, but because God is infinitely gracious. I know some of you are probably thinking, "Well, we can't possibly own everything Jesus does as God." And, I agree that we are not God. We are not made deity through Jesus. But, we do inherit everything He possesses as the perfect God-man.

God has included you in His divine will so that Christ's inheritance has your name on it. This changes everything for us. You're not just another random person. You are a child of God and fellow heir with Jesus. This is the highest position that could ever be granted by God.

There is much more we could say about our identity in Christ, but these are the key attributes that are worth touching on for the sake of this book. Your self-confidence and value should go through the roof now that you know who God has made you to be.

This shouldn't feed your ego or grow your pride. This should leave you humbly on your face before the Lord as you kneel in awe of what He's granted you. The King has extended the ultimate position to us, and He has made us something we never could've become or dreamed up on our own.

And, we don't have to work to maintain this standing before God. It is a free gift that we enjoy. But, this new identity does come with a purpose, and Paul explains this in Ephesians 2:10.

Ephesians 2:10 - For we are his workmanship, **created in Christ Jesus for good works**, *which God prepared beforehand, that we should walk in them.*

God has positioned us for the plans He has prepared for us. He's made us what we need to be in order to accomplish His calling for our life. Before God changes our behavior, He changes who we are.

But, God's purpose for our life involves a process. If we don't understand this divine process, we'll live frustrated, anxious, discouraged or disappointed. This is what we'll discuss next.

Level 3: Process |

Chapter 8: Heart Posture

One of the most important things that God has ever taught me is His divine process.

See, God is moving us towards an ultimate goal, and Jesus is that goal. We're moving towards the culmination of human history where everything in Heaven and earth will be united in Christ.

And, there is a process that God uses to move us in the direction of that goal. Once I understood this, it improved my life dramatically. I'm not exaggerating.

I spent so much of my life believing a false idea about God's process. I expected God to do something He never said He would, and I wasted so much time and energy on a role that God never designed me for.

I knew that God wanted fruit. I knew that He wanted me to image Him well in the earth, but I was trying to do that outside of His perfect process. And, trust me, His process works. His process is the only thing that can accomplish His desired results.

The Divine Process

God desires results that are best for us, so let's breakdown this process simply and biblically.

Here is God's step-by-step process for your life purpose:

1) Seek the Lord
2) Know the Lord
3) Love the Lord
4) Obey the Lord
5) Reflect the Lord
6) Glorify the Lord

God calls us to seek Him, which results in knowing Him and loving Him. As love grows in our hearts, we will walk in growing obedience to God, reflect His glory to the world and glorify Him with our life. This is how God gets things done in the lives of His people.

This might seem basic, but it is actually way more complex than you probably think. And, believe me, this order matters. If you operate outside of this order or try and skip a step, you won't experience the best possible life that God has for you.

Your life won't achieve the same results. God's purpose for your life follows this order and process, so it makes sense that we would do the same.

Chapter 8: Heart Posture

In this chapter, I want to explain this process a bit more in-depth to help you understand what you should be focusing on as a child of God. Not only does the order of God's process matter, but your role in His process matters just as much. We need to learn how to submit to God's process for our life by playing the role He's called us to.

And, just to be clear, God initiated this divine fruit-bearing process in our life by His own grace. He makes this process even possible. He sent His own Son to save us. He became the way when there was no way. He forgives us and fills us with His Spirit.

The second we trust in Jesus, God kickstarts His divine fruit-bearing process in our life. Our faith in Jesus was a decision to step into the river of God's divine plan and process.

God hits the "activate" button, so that we are now in a process that is guaranteed to end in ultimate success. Nothing will stop it. This process is guaranteed to reach completion because of God's grace; not because of our efforts. God's process for our lives has a 100% success rate. In fact, Paul guarantees that God will continue what He starts in His people.

> *Philippians 1:6 - And I am sure of this, that* **he who began a good work in you will bring it to completion** *at the day of Jesus Christ.*

God finishes what He starts in us. But, we still have a responsibility to align ourselves with God's process by submitting to the role He's assigned to us. This passage is not permission to live lazy, inactive and passive. This Scripture should motivate you to go after everything God has for you because of the guaranteed victory and success we have in Christ.

Seek His Face

The first step in this process is seeking the Lord, in order to know Him and love Him.

Knowledge of God produces love for God, but we can't know God if we don't invest into our relationship with Him. It is our job to seek the Lord. He doesn't force us. He encourages, He enables, and He invites us into this relationship He has for us, but it is our personal decision to seek Him or not.

You might make this idea more complicated than it is, so I want you to think of two main things when I say to seek the Lord. First, read/meditate on God's word and second, spend time with God in prayer. These are NOT the only two ways to seek the Lord, but they are the primary ways that we can personally seek the face of God according to Scripture.

Seeking God is the first step to bearing good fruit. Remember, God's goal for your life is that you would bear good fruit by growing in His image, reflecting His image and multiplying His image in others, and that will only happen when you choose to seek God. As you genuinely seek the Lord in prayer and in His word, you'll see good fruit produced naturally in your life.

The word of God plays such a key role in our life, and I want to show you why. God's word is referred to as seed all throughout the Bible, and this is important. Seed produces fruit.

Chapter 8: Heart Posture

*James 1:21 - Therefore put away all filthiness and rampant wickedness and **receive with meekness the implanted word**, which is able to save your souls.*

James tells us that if we humbly receive the implanted word of God, our souls will be saved. The gospel message of Jesus is seed that takes root in our hearts to produce salvation, transformation, and glorification. God's word is supposed to take root in our hearts like seed.

One of Jesus' parables is about a farmer that goes out and scatters seed and the seed falls on four different types of soils. We see this parable in Luke 8:1-18. Jesus says that some of the seed fell on hard ground, some fell on rocky soil, some fell on thorny soil, and some fell on good soil. Out of all four soils, only one soil had seed that produced good fruit.

Jesus explains that the seed represents the word of God, and the farmer represents Jesus, who preaches the word of God. The four kinds of soils represent four types of people who have different heart conditions. Jesus makes it clear that only one kind of person will receive His word and have their life transformed, and that's the person who humbly receives and believes in the gospel message of Jesus.

This parable shows us that the word of God is designed to produce good fruit and transformation in our life. But, our heart posture really affects what happens with that seed. Part of God's divine process includes the condition of our hearts as we receive His word.

So, I want you to really think about this. Whenever you open the Bible, are you positioned to receive the seed of God's word? Is your heart humbly submitted to what God wants to do in your life? Are you open to what God has to say, and are you ready to change however God tells you to?

Fruitfulness happens for those who are positioned to receive the word of God, and James tells us to humbly, receive God's word with meekness. This means you can receive Scripture with a wrong heart that prevents complete fruitfulness.

Your own heart posture can prove to be an obstacle between you and good fruit. So, I want to help you understand how to appropriately seek God in His word.

How you approach the Bible really matters, because your approach will determine the result. It will often determine what you get out of it. So, the results of your time in Scripture will be affected by how you approach His word. This includes your motives, intentions, goals, expectations, and even your view of God's word.

This doesn't mean that you have to be aware of every way that God is working on you through His word in order for anything to happen. God doesn't need your awareness in order to effectively work in your heart. In fact, God works in many ways that we're unaware of, until the fruit is evident.

I just want you to understand that your approach to Scripture can encourage or disrupt what God wants to do in your heart.

For example, if I approach a recipe book as if it is a basic, instructional manual on cooking, I will be very disappointed by the results of my time spent in that recipe book. A recipe book provides formulas, step-by-step instructions and

Chapter 8: Heart Posture

ingredients for specific recipes. A cookbook will provide basic cooking techniques as well as the science behind cooking.

I shouldn't expect a recipe book to teach me basic cooking techniques and the general science behind cooking. A recipe book functions differently than a cookbook, which means that I'm approaching that recipe book improperly. The problem isn't with the author of the recipe book. The issue is my own expectations and approach.

The author of the recipe book wanted me to whip up a certain recipe how they did. They want me to experience the taste, texture and satisfaction of the dish they enjoyed. But, I'm expecting the author to teach me basic cooking instructions and techniques that apply to all types of dishes. I might learn a few cooking techniques and a bit about the science, but my expectations won't be met. No matter how long I spend in that book, I'll be disappointed.

This is how many Christians experience the Bible. They leave their quiet time with the Lord being very disappointed and having unmet expectations. They expected God to accomplish something that He never said He would. And, eventually Christians grow frustrated and discouraged enough to rarely open the Scriptures. This leaves a Christian not having much seed planted in their hearts, which is why they don't experience much good fruit in their life.

Honestly, I know many Christians that stopped spending time in God's word because they've lost motivation over time. And usually that lost motivation is due to a continual experience of unfulfilled expectations, because they repeatedly approached Scripture the wrong way.

Son, Student, And Soldier

So, the big question is, what kind of heart posture should we have when we approach the Bible? There are three key ways you should interact with the word of God. You should approach the Bible as a child, as a scholar, and as a soldier.

Whether you're hearing the preaching of God's word, coming across a daily verse, or reading the Bible on your own, these three mentalities can change everything for you.

In fact, when God first revealed these three ways to approach Scripture, a world of revelation opened up for me. We have to keep in mind that God's word primarily exists to reveal God through a story that spans human history. God uses human authors to write down His story of redemption, and through that story, God is mainly revealing Himself to us.

> *Proverbs 8:17 - I love those who **love me**, and those who **seek me** diligently **find me**.*

According to Proverbs 8:17, we seek the Lord in order to find Him, which is to know Him. This is why we have to approach the Scriptures as a child who just wants to know their Father. Once I understood that the Bible was a unified story that reveals God, I began to read the Bible in order to know Him.

I used to view the Bible as a moral handbook for life. In fact, I've heard some people say that the Bible is our basic instructions before leaving earth. And, that isn't wrong, but it is not a complete answer.

Chapter 8: Heart Posture

The Bible does show us God's moral laws and His standards for our life because these rules show us how to live the best possible life. But, the laws and standards of God are an extension of His own character. They are not separate. We understand God's laws best when we know His heart. This is one of the reasons we should approach the Bible as a child that just wants to spend time with their Father.

God desires for us to know His heart and understand His ways. This is the heart behind the book of Psalms. The Psalmist just desires to spend time in the presence of God where God reveals His ways and His character. We should open the Bible to know our Father, not simply to know more facts.

Information is fine as long as it leads to transformation. But, transformation only happens when we've encountered God, which happens primarily through His living word.

Think of it like this. If God offered you the chance to legitimately look into His divine throne room, would you take His offer? Think of certain Old Testament saints who had the privilege of seeing God in a unique way that no one else was able to. They longed to see the radiant majesty of the living God, and God answered their desire.

If God made that offer to me, there's no way I would miss a chance to visibly, physically see His glory and majesty with my own eyes.

God is inviting us to spiritually see Him when we read the Bible. He isn't simply giving us some helpful boundaries for our life. He isn't just giving us a handful of rules that improve our life. He isn't just telling us how to avoid judgment. The triune God is inviting us to come and know Him through the window of Scripture.

The word of God should be seen as a window into the throne room of Heaven, where we get a personal glimpse of the Almighty God. But, how many people approach the Bible in order to encounter and know God in a personal way?

So, as you seek the Lord, make sure your heart is mainly set on knowing His heart, not just experiencing His blessings. I've heard it said that we should seek the face of God more than we seek His hand. God's presence has more value in my life than anything He can give me. Open the Scriptures as a child who just wants to be with their Father.

There are times when my son is hanging out with me and he just has this look of complete enjoyment and satisfaction on his face. We might not be doing anything particularly fun or special, but he seems so content. Often, he will even say "dad I just love being with you." In that moment, he enjoys my presence so much that he has to express the pleasure and joy he's feeling.

This is what I imagine God desires of us as we enjoy spending time with Him in His word. We need to be more childlike when we open the Bible and not be so overly-intellectual.

But, this doesn't mean we approach the Bible mindlessly without any sense of intelligence. Some people think the Bible is a supernatural book that doesn't involve our intellect.

But, the second way we approach the Bible is as a student that wants to understand the deep mysteries and wisdom of

Chapter 8: Heart Posture

God. This means critical thinking, logic, and thoughtful meditation are involved in reading the Bible.

But, this doesn't mean that God's ability to transform you is limited to your own knowledge or intelligence. He reveals spiritual truth through His Spirit, but that process involves some responsibility on our end.

> **John 16:13** - When the Spirit of truth comes, **he will guide you into all the truth**, for he will not speak on his own authority, but whatever he hears he will speak, and he will declare to you the things that are to come.

The Spirit of God leads and guides us into the truth, but this assumes that we're positioned to be led into the truth. Part of this means that we're submitted to the leading of God's Spirit and part of this means that we're doing our part to arrive at the truth of God. This is actually best seen in Acts 17 when the Bereans are receiving the word of God while examining the truthfulness of what Paul is saying. They listen with an open Bible.

> Acts 17:10-11 - The brothers immediately sent Paul and Silas away by night to Berea, and when they arrived they went into the Jewish synagogue. Now these Jews were more noble than those in Thessalonica; **they received the word with all eagerness**, examining the Scriptures daily to see if these things were so.

The Bereans weren't mindlessly receiving everything Paul said, but they weren't opposed to what he said either. They had open hearts that were eager to receive what Paul was saying, but simultaneously, they were examining their own

Scriptures to see if Paul was telling the truth. This is a great example of what it means to be a humble student of Scripture.

So, what does it mean to be a student of Scripture? When we read the Bible, we're supposed to meditate on what we're reading. We're supposed to think through the implications of a passage and how our life should change. There should be logical reasoning involved where we consider how to make sense of what we're reading. We should critically think through how a passage connects to the rest of Scripture.

We should ask questions. We should really think through what a passage means by examining things like the grammatical context, literary context, and historical context. We want to understand God's intended meaning, and this involves thoughtful meditation.

Think of someone that has dedicated their life to being a student. They love learning and they spend most of their time in the library. They always have a book in their hand because they've decided to spend their life pursuing knowledge.

Sometimes you see them pause to think through what they just read in order to make sense of it. They don't move on to the next page until they understand what's right in front of them. They're taking notes and desiring to learn. Good students don't just read books to memorize information for a test. They read to understand and learn for the rest of their life.

This is what it looks like to approach the Bible as a student. Not only do we desire to know our Father, but we are faithful students of God's word. We've decided to seek out the secret knowledge and wisdom of God that He reveals through His Spirit. We should desire to understand God's intended meaning behind any biblical passage.

The goal is to know the Father, but the process to knowing Him actually involves thoughtful meditation, critical thinking, and praying through the Scripture. We can't apply something we don't understand.

I remember in my first year as a youth pastor, I had some students that were proud of how much of the Bible they were reading in one sitting. They'd tell me how they read ten chapters at a time as if that was an accomplishment.

But, then I'd ask what they read about or what they learned, and they usually couldn't remember. They'd absorbed so much information but they didn't understand any of it. They didn't apply any of it. I'd ask them how helpful it was that they read tons of Scripture if they didn't apply or understand any of it.

This is what I want to ask you. When you read the Bible, are you more concerned about filling your brain with as much information as possible? Or, are you more concerned with understanding and applying whatever you're reading, even if its just a few verses?

Jesus would define faithfulness as living out what you learn. Faithfulness isn't based solely on what you know, it's based on what you do with what you know. It isn't about the amount. God is concerned with the quality of our understanding and whether or not our life changes at all.

The third way we should approach the Bible is as a soldier. As we seek to know our Father as a child, and as we seek to understand His word as a student, we should also be aware that the word of God is changing us into the image of Jesus for the sake of our daily battle with sin.

> *2 Timothy 3:16-17 - All Scripture is breathed out by God and profitable for teaching, for reproof, for correction, and **for training in righteousness**, that the man of God may be complete, **equipped** for every good work.*

The word of God is training us in righteousness the way a soldier is trained up to be capable of doing his job in warfare. The word of God is equipping us for everything God wants to bring us into. We are soldiers of God being trained up in His word for battle.

We are in the midst of spiritual warfare constantly. And, the word of God is preparing us for the daily warfare we engage in. The Scriptures actually equip and train us to do battle with sin, the flesh, and the powers of darkness.

As we read the Bible, we're growing in strength, endurance, confidence, and developing the abilities necessary to do warfare as a faithful soldier. The Bible becomes a sort of training grounds to develop soldiers of God. The word of God acts as our spiritual gym.

When I read the Bible, I picture God transporting me to His heavenly training grounds where He's developing my skills and ability to effectively do battle with the enemy. Some might even say reading the Bible is a form of spiritual warfare.

Either way, our time in God's word is related to our spiritual battles. Scripture sets us up for victory in spiritual warfare.

So many people forget about spiritual warfare when they approach the Bible. But, as we're meeting with God in His word, God is mindful of every future battle we'll encounter, and He's preparing us accordingly. We must have this mindset when we approach the Bible.

God is raising up His army of soldiers who will do battle everyday, but this soldier mentality shouldn't prevent us from enjoying the presence of God as a child or learning as a faithful student. These three mentalities should work together when we read the Bible.

So, as we unpack God's process for His people, we have to remember that God's primary method of growth and transformation is His word that is applied by His Spirit. Jesus says this exact thing in John 17:17 where He prays to the Father that He might sanctify His people in His word.

> *John 17:17 - Sanctify them **in the truth**; your word is truth.*

God is the master potter who is forming us into the image of Jesus. And, what is God's main tool? His word is. The word of God is sculpting us and shaping us into the likeness of Jesus. Peter confirms that Scripture is an important element in God's process for our life.

> *2 Peter 3:18 - But **grow** in the grace and knowledge of our Lord and Savior Jesus Christ. To him be the glory both now and to the day of eternity. Amen.*

*1 Peter 2:2-3 - Like newborn infants, long for the pure spiritual milk, that by it you may **grow** up into salvation— 3 if indeed you have tasted that the Lord is good.*

God is bringing us through a process of supernatural growth and transformation. We are on a journey of producing good fruit for God's glory, and Peter says that we grow up into fruitfulness as we grow in the knowledge of our God. This requires us to spend time in His word in order to know Him. As we just spend time with our Father in His word, He grows us.

God's word is the only way that we will bear good fruit. Lasting transformation and spiritual growth will not happen apart from the word of God. But, how we approach God's word matters, because our approach affects the outcome of our Bible study.

As we approach God's word with the right heart, we are positioning ourselves for optimal growth and transformation. When we approach Scripture as a child, a student, and a soldier, we're positioning our heart to be receptive to the work God wants to accomplish in our lives.

So, before you even open the Scripture, I want you to learn to ask yourself, "Am I positioned for fruit?"

All you're asking is whether or not your heart is receptive to the work that God intends to accomplish in your life. We want to have hearts that are capable of receiving the word of God as well as the transformation He wants to bring in our life.

Chapter 8: Heart Posture

Colossians 1:10 - *So as to walk in a manner worthy of the Lord, fully pleasing to him,* **bearing fruit in every good work** *and increasing in the knowledge of God*

As we are seeking the Lord in His word and in prayer, God is accomplishing His divine process in our life. But, at the same time Colossians 1:10 says that it is our responsibility to increase in the knowledge of God as we're living a life that is worthy of the Lord.

We are the lives that bear good fruit, but it is God who produces that fruit in our life. He makes good fruit possible, which is absolutely essential for us to understand.

God handles the fruit as we position our lives for optimal fruitfulness. It is our job to seek the Lord and increase in the knowledge of our God. And, as we do, God accomplishes the impossible in our life. I want to bring us back to 2 Peter for a minute to show you how simple God has made this process for us. God could not have made His divine process more simple.

> *2 Peter 1:2-3 - May grace and peace be multiplied to you in the knowledge of God and of Jesus our Lord.* 3 **His divine power has granted to us all things** *that pertain to life and godliness, through the knowledge of him who called us to his own glory and excellence*

Peter says that God's power has granted to us ALL THINGS that we need to live a life of Godliness. In other words, God has given us absolutely everything we need to live the fullest life and accomplish our God-given purpose. We are well-equipped. But, then Peter says all of these resources we need are available in the knowledge of Jesus.

So, how does God supply us what we need? Through the knowledge of Him which is found in His word. How does God equip us with everything required to accomplish His purpose for our life? He supplies these things through His word.

God's delivery system is His word. His Spirit delivers us our divine blessings in the packaging of Scripture. If you want to see your life accomplish everything God has for you, it requires you to know God in His word.

Your job in this process is to seek the Lord and know Him, and He will accomplish everything you can't. We do what we can, and God does what we can't. He's made it so simple.

Level 3: Process

Chapter 9: Just Abide

This just might be the most important chapter in this book. I'm not exaggerating. So far, we've examined our purpose, our position, and part of our role in God's process. God calls us to seek Him faithfully with the right heart, and as we do, God will handle everything else.

We've examined the first three steps in God's process, which is to seek God, know Him and love Him. But, there is a dimension of that third step that we need to examine. I didn't fully unpack the concept of our love for God, so I want to briefly touch on our love for God in order to move into the other steps in God's process.

Many Christians have this idea that they need to force love for God. They're under the impression that love is something we accomplish in our own strength by our own efforts. But, love is not something we can manufacture. This doesn't mean that we don't have a responsibility to choose to love God. Love is a choice, so we definitely choose to love God.

But, how is this love for God actually realized? How does love happen in our lives? The answer is in 1 John 4:19.

*1 John 4:19 - We love **because he first loved us.***

Our love is responsive, which means that our love for God is actually a response to His love for us. He initiated this process by choosing to love us first, and His love is what awakens love in us. Paul puts it another way in Galatians 5.

*Galatians 5:22 -But **the fruit of the Spirit is love**, joy, peace, patience, kindness, goodness, faithfulness.*

Paul says that love is actually the fruit of the Spirit. We've already discussed that fruit comes from seed, which means that love is produced in us by the Spirit of God through the seed of His word. God's word is the seed that results in the fruit of love. So, our love for God is the result of His word taking root in our hearts.

And, remember that our love is in response to God's love for us. So, the better we know and understand His love, the more love we will have for God and people who bear His image. His love is revealed in His word, which means we need to know His word to have love for Him.

With that in mind, I want to show you the nature of God's process a bit more in depth. I want to give you understanding of how God's process logistically works. See, I'm a nerd. I like to know how things work because that understanding becomes my power.

I believe this is true of God's process for our life. God has invited us into His divine process, not just to participate in it but to understand His ways as well. I don't just want to tell you what to do, and I don't just want to tell you why you should do it.

God's Process Works

If you can understand how God's process logistically works, you'll likely have more motivation to do what He's called you to. Even though God doesn't reveal every detail to us, He reveals enough for us. So, what is our role in God's process? God primarily calls us to seek Him, but Jesus explains this idea a bit more in-depth in John 15.

> John 15:4 - **Abide in me, and I in you**. *As the branch cannot bear fruit by itself, unless it abides in the vine, neither can you, unless you abide in me.*

In this passage, Jesus is just hours away from being arrested and crucified. His disciples are confused and deeply hurt. Jesus wants to share some last words that will encourage and comfort His disciples through everything that is about to happen.

Of all the things Jesus could say, He tells His disciples to abide in Him. Why does He command this one main thing? Because it works.

Abiding in Jesus has a 100% success rate of producing good fruit in our lives. Remember, there is a system that God has put in place, and God's system works 100% of the time. This is a process God has put in place to progress His people towards fruitfulness. We've discussed it briefly in the last chapter, but look at it one more time.

Here is God's step-by-step process for your life purpose:

1) Seek the Lord
2) Know the Lord
3) Love the Lord
4) Obey the Lord
5) Reflect the Lord
6) Glorify the Lord

Jesus gives His disciples one key responsibility. This is the one thing He tells them to do, and everything else will follow. He tells them to abide in Him. This involves seeking the Lord, like we've discussed already. But, there is more. God's divine process or "system" is centered around this idea of abiding in Jesus. It's as if God's process for your life is built on this one main concept of abiding. So, we have to rightly define what this means.

The Greek word for abide is "meinate" and this word literally means to remain, continue, stay, or wait. Here's what this means for us. Abide means to stay close to Jesus through our continual believing loyalty, trust, obedience, and seeking.

Our job is to continue believing in His word, trusting in His promises, obeying His commands and seeking His presence in order to stay as close to Him as possible. This is a life that is spent waiting on the Lord in faith.

This means we're continuing to trust in the gospel by maintaining faith in the promises of God, and as we continue believing, this will translate into a more passionate pursuit of the Lord. While we do this, we'll experience a growing knowledge of God and obedience to Him.

Chapter 9: Just Abide

This doesn't mean that you stay close to Jesus in order to stay saved and forgiven. We don't maintain our salvation by our own good deeds and obedience. But, I will say that lifelong faith is a mark of a true believer. This means that someone who is saved and forgiven will stay close to Jesus.

Let me illustrate this.

Think of a rollercoaster, or any kind of ride at a theme park. Usually, a rollercoaster will have a harness that comes over you to strap you in securely. You're safe during the ride because the harness secures you. But, there are also usually handle bars on the shoulder harness for you to hold onto. During certain moments throughout the ride, you may cling tighter to that harness, but you're not secure because of your death grip on the harness.

You're secure because of the harness that straps you into the ride. You might cling tighter to the harness but that's only because you're strapped in securely. In other words, you are clinging tighter to what secures you during the crazy ride. Your efforts and strength to hang on is not what secures you; the harness secures you.

This is the Christian life. We abide in Jesus not to be any more secure or safe from the wrath of God. We abide in Jesus and cling to Him because He is the One that has already secured our soul. Our abiding is not what secures us. Abiding is what proves genuine faith in Jesus.

What I want you to really understand is that God commands us to abide in Him as our main responsibility. We just abide while God handles the outcome. Let me explain with John 15.

> John 15:4-5 - *Abide in me, and I in you. As the branch cannot bear fruit by itself, unless it abides in the vine, neither can you, unless you abide in me. 5 I am the vine; you are the branches.* **Whoever abides in me and I in him, he it is that bears much fruit, for apart from me you can do nothing.**

We've already briefly discussed that good fruit is impossible apart from Jesus. This is why Jesus commands His disciples to abide. Jesus is the vine that makes His branches fruitful, but only a branch that remains connected to Jesus will bear good fruit.

This is why Jesus addresses the lifeless, barren, severed branches later in John 15.

Understanding Fruitfulness

> John 15:6 - **If anyone does not abide in me he is thrown away** *like a branch and withers; and the branches are gathered, thrown into the fire, and burned.*

Many people take this verse to mean that people who don't continue abiding will end up losing their precious salvation and friendship with God. But, Jesus is actually making a reference to unbelieving Israelites who have experienced a national closeness to the God of Israel through their sacrificial system, temple, Mosaic law, and established religious system.

These Israelites were connected to the God of Israel through their physical descent from Abraham. But, just like Paul makes clear in Romans 11, many Israelites were cut off from the Kingdom of God, in the sense that they were exposed as

Chapter 9: Just Abide

never being spiritually connected to the God of Israel. They never had believing loyalty to the God of Israel.

Many unbelieving Jews merely appeared to have a connection to the God of Israel when in fact they had no living, abiding relationship with God. This is especially true of Judas, who coincidentally has just left to betray Jesus moments before Jesus shares these words in John 15.

So, what I understand of this biblical passage is that branches that don't bear good fruit didn't lose their salvation, but they proved they never had genuine faith. Their barrenness proves that they never truly trusted in God for salvation and forgiveness of sins.

Someone who lives a life of continual sin with moments of "goodness" reveals the sad reality that they don't have a real, abiding relationship with God, otherwise they would continue to bear good fruit. So, abiding is not the requirement to get into Heaven. Faith in Jesus is the requirement. But, abiding is the necessary evidence that proves someone has real, saving faith.

So, according to Jesus in John 15, there are not categories of Christians. There are two categories of people on the earth. There are fruitful branches that abide in Jesus, and there are fruitless branches that are disconnected from Christ through their unbelief and unrepentant heart.

I want to repeat myself so you understand: abiding and bearing good fruit are not the requirements for being a Christian. Rather, those are the results of being a Christian. This is what happens organically. A child of God will be enabled by the grace of God and the Holy Spirit to live a life of continual, believing loyalty where they are bearing good fruit.

Here's what I want to pause and say to you directly: stop obsessing over the fruit and begin focusing more on the root. The root of our salvation and Christian faith is King Jesus. The root that produces good fruit is Jesus. The good fruit we'll experience in our life is a result of abiding in Jesus. We are the branches that stay close through growing obedience, faith, and knowledge, and Jesus is the vine that makes us fruitful.

> *Philippians 1:9-11 - And it is my prayer that your love may abound more and more, with knowledge and all discernment, so that you may approve what is excellent, and so be pure and blameless for the day of Christ,* **filled with the fruit of righteousness that comes through Jesus Christ**, *to the glory and praise of God.*

In the mind of Paul, the fruit of righteousness comes through Jesus Christ who fills us with these good fruits. So, who is credited with the good fruit in our lives? Jesus is credited!

Guaranteed, But Not Immediate

Now that we understand the concept of abiding, I want to blow your mind the way God has blown my mind over the years with this passage. When you truly understand these basic truths, everything in your life can change forever.

Chapter 9: Just Abide

I'll continue to reference John 15 in order to reinforce what I'm telling you, so maybe bookmark that passage in your Bible as you read through the rest of this chapter.

In John 15, Jesus says that His disciples are guaranteed to bear good fruit in their life if they just abide in Him. And, abiding is not a one-time action, but a lifelong decision. Sure, we commit our lives to Jesus in one moment for salvation, but abiding and seeking Jesus is an everyday decision we make for the rest of our life.

You don't choose to abide in Jesus and seek Him one time as if that's enough for the rest of your life. You will continue abiding for the rest of your life because you can always grow closer to God. Abiding is lifelong and everyday.

> *Luke 9:23 - And he said to all, "If anyone would come after me, let **him deny himself and take up his cross daily and follow me**.*

Jesus emphasizes the daily need for His disciples to deny themselves, and continue following Him even into the most uncomfortable and painful situations. Faith is lifelong or it wasn't genuine. This means that every day Jesus calls us to follow Him and deny ourselves.

Now, this doesn't mean we will always, perfectly abide in Jesus, but the majority of our life will be marked by abiding in Him. There will be moments, days and even seasons where we don't abide in Jesus the way we should, the way we have before, or even sometimes we won't choose to abide at all because of our flesh.

Everyday we will likely experience a different degree of abiding in Jesus. We should ask God to make us more consistent, but we shouldn't be overcome by shame and disappointment.

So, Jesus guarantees good fruit for those who abide in Him. It is automatic. This is one of those absolutes in the universe that God has divinely set in place. As surely as the sun will rise, a child of God that abides in Jesus will most certainly bear good fruit.

But, here's what I wish someone told me as a younger Christian: good fruit is guaranteed for those who abide in Jesus, but it won't be immediate. And, that good fruit isn't according to our preference.

When you hear that God promises good fruit for those who abide in Him, you might be tempted to believe that this means you'll see good fruit produced immediately. We often believe the lie that we know better than God. So, we begin assuming that we know best about how good fruit should be produced in our lives.

We assume God is going to bear fruit in our lives the way we want Him to.

We assume that God's process will be according to our timing and preferred methods. We even assume that good fruit will look a certain way. When we hear "good fruit" we picture a certain amount of fruit, a specific size, and even the kind of fruit it will be.

Chapter 9: Just Abide

But, abiding doesn't guarantee the kind of good fruit you prefer. Abiding guarantees the kind of fruit God knows you need at the exact time God knows is best. I had to learn to sacrifice my own concept of time, my preferences, and my idea of what good fruit would even look like.

For example, I found myself praying for God to increase my purity and remove lust from my heart, and this was the main kind of "good fruit" I desired for God to produce in my life. I imagined that God would do it immediately, because He's all-powerful, so, of course He should. I pictured God removing lust completely and replacing it with complete purity.

But, I failed to acknowledge God's process for producing good fruit in the life of His people.

After several months of praying this prayer, I got frustrated, because I expected immediate results that looked a certain way. Not only did I hold God hostage to my timing and method but I held Him hostage to my preferred outcome.

God had a different process in mind, though.

Over time I realized that God was answering my prayer a different way than I had imagined. God was indirectly addressing my purity and lust issues by growing my self control and discipline in other areas of my life. And, I didn't realize this, but these seemingly unrelated areas of my life actually had deep connections to my own lack of sexual purity.

Even if I had realized this immediately after praying, I didn't see the evidence of this self control growing in the garden of my heart until after several months of seeking the Lord faithfully and continuing to abide in Him.

Once I saw these fruits growing in my life, I slowly began to realize that God was addressing my cry for purity by providing me self control to resist sexual temptation. I was learning that God controls the fruit that results from my abiding, not me. My job is to trust He knows what kind of good fruit needs to be produced and He knows what pace of growth is best.

Think about a garden. When you plant seed in the soil, you don't see evidence of its growth until it begins sprouting out of the soil. There is a time period between planting and seeing evidence of growth. And, while you see no visible evidence of growth above the surface, there is a ton of growth taking place underground that only God sees.

This is exactly what happens in the garden of our hearts when we abide and continue seeking the Lord in His word and prayer. God is planting seeds, watering, and causing growth to happen at the optimal pace. God sets the pace of our growth and He determines what grows in our heart garden.

If you could see my heart during the months I was praying for purity, you'd see that God was planting different seeds than I had imagined. He was growing self control rather than purity, but He knew this process was best for His calling on my life. He knew that self control and discipline were necessary for other areas of my life that He was improving, but also that this would eventually affect the purity that I had been praying for.

You might be wondering why God chose to take so long to grow this specific good fruit in the garden of my heart. And,

Chapter 9: Just Abide

I just want to say that God is in no rush. He exists outside of time, while we're bound by time. While we're obsessed with the goal and the outcome, God is more concerned with the process we go through to arrive at our desired outcome.

When we pray for specific good fruit in our life, we can think of these requests as goals. But, there is a journey to these destinations. There is a process God takes us through in order to develop in us what we need for the things He's called us to. We are so one-track-minded. We only focus on one main area of our life and pray for that specific area, but God sees how every area of our life connects to millions of other moments that relate to His Kingdom.

While we abide, we need to learn to trust that God knows best about what to do through our decision to abide. He knows best how to lead us to our desired good fruits, and He knows what needs to be developed along the way.

This understanding freed me from the illusion of control that I had. I was remaining close to Jesus while trying to control the kind of fruit that was produced through my obedience. I was doing my part while trying to do God's part, but we have to learn to trust God with His part. Real trust in God allows us to play our role faithfully in the midst of uncertainty.

The fact is, I have no idea what God is doing deep in my heart as I seek Him in His word and prayer. It isn't always apparent or completely evident. We need to abandon the lie that we know what God should be doing in our hearts as we abide in Him. We don't know best, but our God does. This doesn't mean that we can't pray for certain kind of good fruit, and it doesn't mean that we shouldn't expect God to answer our prayers for specific good fruit.

God's Responsibility Is Fruit

I just want you to understand that good fruit is not your responsibility. Your responsibility is to abide and trust God with the outcome. God's job is to handle the outcome, but your job is to abide. This is the main thing Jesus commands His disciples to do.

And, as you do your job, God will do His job by producing the good fruit in your life that He knows you need. God is in charge of the pace of growth as well as the method He chooses to produce growth in our lives.

I'll say it another way for some that still don't see it.

God doesn't command you to control the fruit you produce, He commands you to abide. This doesn't mean that God doesn't expect good fruit from His people. He just knows that we don't control the fruit production in our life.

We control whether or not we'll position our lives for fruitfulness by abiding in Jesus or not. Our job is to encourage good fruit in our life, not control what fruit is produced or how quickly we experience growth.

You might be abiding in Jesus and expecting God to produce specific good fruit in your life. But, He is the vinedresser, not us. We just abide. Once I understood that this was my responsibility, I felt a burden lift off of my life.

Chapter 9: Just Abide

So many people are anxious and worried because they've assumed a role that God never told them to. You can't be both the branch and the vinedresser. As long as you're trying to control the outcome of your abiding, you will find yourself discouraged, anxious, worried and even depressed.

You either trust God to take care of you as you faithfully abide in Jesus, or you don't trust Him.

I'll say it another way and back this all up with Scripture.

You aren't in control of how you grow or when you grow. Your spiritual growth is God's job, because He is the only One that can actually make anything grow.

You don't control what specific good fruit grows in the garden of your heart. You just cultivate your heart garden to be ideal for good fruit or bad fruit to grow. I only say this to help you understand you role so you can live in the fullness of joy that God has made available to you.

> 1 Corinthians 3:7 - So neither he who plants nor he who waters is anything, **but only God who gives the growth**.

Paul makes it clear that no one can be credited with the fruit of salvation except God, because He alone gives the growth. This is specifically talking about saving faith growing in a person's heart, but the concept remains true for all people.

God makes things grow, and this is good news that we will discuss further in the next chapter.

Level 3: Process |
Chapter 10: Controlled Fruit

Psalm 127:1 - **Unless the LORD builds the house**, *those who build it labor in vain.* **Unless the LORD watches over the city**, *the watchman stays awake in vain.*

Humans can work tirelessly to build something, but without God's sovereign hand guiding the process, their efforts will be useless. This one verse puts finite, limited humans in their place. I know this verse has personally done it for me.

Sometimes we can get caught up in the false idea that our efforts will produce a guaranteed outcome because the universe is supposed to work like that. But, the only real absolutes in the universe are what God has eternally promised in His word.

The very planet we live on, is not as reliable as the word of God according to Jesus' own words in Matthew 24.

Matthew 24:35 - Heaven and earth **will pass away**, *but my words will* **not pass away**.

Chapter 10: Controlled Fruit

Heaven and earth will pass away, but God's word will not. The word of God is more reliable than the oxygen we are breathing, the ground we're standing on, and the gravity holding us down.

We shouldn't assume that our spiritual efforts are guaranteed to produce our preferred outcome when our very universe is only as reliable as God allows it to be. The laws that govern our universe will eventually be proven to be temporary, which means that the lesser things within our universe must be even less reliable.

But, anything that God has declared in His word will most certainly happen, even within our fading universe.

We Can Do "Nothing"

In the last chapter, we established that we are called to abide. We are not capable of controlling the fruit that is produced through our abiding. We don't control the outcome of our obedience and faithfulness. Our job is simply to abide.

But, I'd like to elaborate a bit more on this concept to give you deep understanding about your role in God's divine process. Let's go back to John 15.

> John 15:5 - *I am the vine; you are the branches. Whoever abides in me and I in him, he it is that bears much fruit, for **apart from me you can do nothing**.*

Jesus makes it clear that His disciples can do nothing apart from Him. But, what does this mean? I know you're probably thinking of unbelievers in your life that have accomplished much. Many unbelievers have tons of money, great accomplishments, and can even achieve success in almost everything they put their mind to.

I won't deny the fact that people can reject Jesus and still achieve great things in this life without following God. So, if unbelievers can be some of the most flourishing, successful people on the planet, what does it mean that we can do nothing apart from Jesus?

In John 15, Jesus defines success as fruitfulness. Bearing good fruit and honoring God is true success that actually lasts forever. The good fruit that God produces in our life will last into eternity, while everything an unbeliever is achieving in this life will eventually amount to nothing. None of their achievements and success will matter when they stand before God on the day of judgment.

It will be as if their life didn't matter at all, because Jesus says apart from Him the best we can do is nothing.

The absence of good fruit is "nothing." So, when Jesus says that we can do "nothing" apart from Him, He means that without Him, our lives aren't capable of doing anything that matters in eternity. Our lives amount to nothing.

Unbelievers might gain much in this life but it is nothing of eternal value. When God looks at a life that isn't bearing good fruit, He sees a life that is accomplishing nothing.

This might sound harsh, but God is looking for good fruit that glorifies His name. We need to re-define success so that we are pursuing those things that God actually cares about.

Chapter 10: Controlled Fruit

Pause, and ask yourself if you are going after things that God cares about. Do you have God's priorities, or are you spending your life doing what God would call "nothing?"

Remember, "nothing" is anything we do that doesn't honor God, or anything we do that violates His word or His character. Whatever we do without the leading of God's Spirit is nothing, because is is the Spirit who makes anything we do amount to something.

I just want you to understand that we can do nothing of eternal value without Jesus, and I'll say it a million different ways until it clicks for you. This revelation has fundamentally changed my life and I want it to change yours. Our human efforts, wisdom, strength, and ability will not produce anything of eternal value without the empowering work of God's Spirit within us.

So, this truth is applicable for both unbelievers and believers. Sure, an unbeliever's entire life will produce nothing of eternal value without Christ. But, at any given moment a Christian can do "nothing" by choosing not to follow God's Spirit in that moment. This means that as we abide in Jesus, it is the Spirit of God that accomplishes anything of eternal value in our lives.

This does't mean we have no responsibility when it comes to bearing good fruit. But, this does mean that God participates with us by His Spirit to enable fruitfulness in our lives. We are His vessel, but He is the power.

God gets the credit and the glory for whatever our life accomplishes but we have the honor of participating in God's eternal plan by choosing to be a willing vessel.

In the last chapter, I said that God is the one who makes things grow. We can work tirelessly and do everything that is "supposed to work," but if God's hand is not on our efforts, nothing will grow. Haggai 1 supports this strongly.

> *Haggai 1:6, 9 -* **You have sown much, and harvested little. You eat, but you never have enough; you drink, but you never have your fill. You clothe yourselves, but no one is warm. And he who earns wages does so to put them into a bag with holes.** *"Thus says the Lord of hosts: Consider your ways. Go up to the hills and bring wood and build the house, that I may take pleasure in it and that I may be glorified, says the Lord.* **You looked for much, and behold, it came to little. And when you brought it home, I blew it away**. *Why? declares the Lord of hosts. Because of my house that lies in ruins, while each of you busies himself with his own house.*

Haggai tells God's people that they have worked very hard to sow seed for a harvest, but they're harvesting only a little. They assumed their efforts would produce a guaranteed outcome, because in their minds, sowing seed guaranteed a plentiful harvest.

But, what they forgot was that God determines whether something grows or not. He decides how much something grows because He alone brings the rain that promotes the growth of seed.

Chapter 10: Controlled Fruit

Then, Haggai tells the Israelites that they eat and drink but its never enough. But, food and drink are supposed to satisfy our bodily hunger and thirst, right? No, food and water don't satisfy. God satisfies. But, God often uses water and food to satisfy. Food and water are not the source of our satisfaction but instead, they are God's methods of bringing satisfaction to His people. God satisfies, not His supply method.

Haggai goes on to say that they are earning money but its as if they're putting their money into bags with holes because it amounts to nothing. The Israelites are doing everything they've done in the past, but they're experiencing an entirely different outcome. And, God tells them why through the prophet Haggai.

God says that their efforts aren't producing the desired outcome, because He's the One determining so. He is doing this because they've neglected the things of God and His Kingdom by choosing to ignore the re-building of His temple.

They've busied themselves with their own profit to the point that they neglect the things of God, and God responds by withholding their preferred outcome.

I want you to see, that as we pursue God and abide in Christ, it is God who is overseeing and determining the outcome of our efforts. He is sovereignly deciding the results of our efforts. Again, we don't decide what is produced from our faithfulness. God does. Our job is to obey, and God's job is to handle the outcome of our obedience.

Sadly, many Christians don't live by this principle. They just assume that if they do the right thing and use the right formula, they will experience a guaranteed outcome. They treat God like a cosmic soda machine, where if they just put in the right amount of quarters, they'll get whatever they want.

But, as I've been saying, God determines the outcome of our efforts. He decides whether our efforts will amount to anything of eternal value. God decides if our labor produces growth or success, and He determines the level to which we'll experience these things.

Once I understood that God controls the fruit of our lives, this allowed me to really enjoy walking with Him without stressing about how my obedience would work out. Since I don't decide the outcome of my efforts, I may as well enjoy the Lord as I do what I know He's given me control over. We control whether or not we'll abide and trust Him with the outcome.

Don't Stop Abiding

*Galatians 6:9 - And let us not grow weary of doing good, for in due season **we will reap**, if we do not give up.*

In Galatians 6, Paul tells the Galatian Christians not to get tired of doing good, because they will eventually reap the fruit of their faithfulness. But it's taking much longer than they'd prefer. Paul tells God's people not to grow discouraged just because they aren't seeing immediate results. He's encouraging God's people by telling them that they will eventually experience the fullness of eternal life in God's presence. This is guaranteed.

Chapter 10: Controlled Fruit

But, Paul is also telling these Christians not to lose heart just because their efforts aren't producing their preferred results according to their preferred time. These Galatian Christians have been doing good, but they aren't experiencing immediate good fruit. It's taking more time than they'd like.

But, God promises that they will reap the good fruit of their faithfulness which is the fullness of eternal life in God's presence forever. Good fruit is guaranteed, but it doesn't always happen as quickly as we prefer.

Sometimes growth is a lot slower than we'd like, and good fruit takes more time than we'd prefer. Often, the process of waiting is exactly what multiplies the fruit God is producing in our lives. As we continue faithfully tending to the Kingdom of God and trusting God with the results, God multiplies the fruit in our lives through the process of waiting for the fruit we've been praying for.

The question is, will you continue abiding in Jesus even though you aren't seeing immediate results? When you experience unfulfilled expectations, can you continue remaining faithful to God? These are questions I have to ask myself constantly.

If God is sovereignly in charge of the results, then I shouldn't conditionally abide as long as I know I'll experience my preferred outcome. We should abide because we love and value Jesus, even if we don't see the immediate results we desire.

Our decision to abide in Jesus, shouldn't be based on the outcome. It should be based on our love for Jesus. But, the good thing is that God promises results. He promises that He will produce good fruit through His people, but He doesn't give specific details about what that will look like for each person.

Can you continue abiding in Jesus even though you don't know the specifics about what God will produce through your faithfulness? In the midst of uncertainty, will you continue abiding in Jesus while you trust Him with the outcome?

> *James 5:7-8 - Be patient, therefore, brothers, until the coming of the Lord. See how the farmer waits for* ***the precious fruit of the earth****, being patient about it, until it receives the early and the late rains. You also, be patient. Establish your hearts, for the coming of the Lord is at hand.*

James, the brother of Jesus, tells God's people to be patient like a farmer. We are waiting for the "precious fruit of the earth" which is the coming of Jesus. As we're waiting for that ultimate priority, we are waiting for other lesser things in this life. Christians require patience, as they wait for the coming of Jesus. And, James chooses to illustrate this patience with a farmer that is waiting for his crops to grow.

A farmer doesn't plant seed and then stare at the soil every second of everyday. The farmer gets to work on other things while the planted seeds are growing, because the farmer knows that he can only do so much to promote the growth of the seeds.

A farmer will daily do his part to promote growth, but he doesn't control growth. He cannot speed up growth past the point that nature allows. And, this is what I want you to realize.

Chapter 10: Controlled Fruit

Even though you don't control growth in your life, you can choose to create an environment that promotes growth in your heart. You can be a patient farmer that tends to the seeds God has planted in your heart while you trust God to bring the best possible growth. You can remove those things that stunt growth. You can get around Godly people that water the seeds that God has planted. You can do all kinds of things that encourage good fruit in your life.

> *Galatians 6:7-8 - Do not be deceived: God is not mocked, for **whatever one sows, that will he also reap**. For the one who sows to his own flesh will from the flesh reap corruption, but the one who sows to the Spirit will from the Spirit reap eternal life.*

You might not control the fruit that is produced in your life, but you control the seeds that are planted in your heart. Paul tells the Galatian church that they decide whether they will plant seeds that produce corruption and destruction or seeds that produce eternal life.

This tells us that believers will spend the majority of their lives planting good seed in their hearts while unbelievers spend their lives planting bad seed in their lives. And, what we have to understand is that we will eat the fruit of our decisions. We will reap the results of what we invest into and plant in the garden of our hearts.

A believer might not be going to hell because they have God's seed abiding in Him, but they can still choose to plant bad seeds in their hearts at any given moment. Seeds are planted in our hearts by what we listen to, watch, engage in, and hang around.

We have to constantly evaluate who and what we're allowing to plant seeds in our hearts because those seeds will eventually turn into fruit that we have to deal with.

So, I don't want you thinking that you have absolutely zero responsibility when it comes to the good fruit that God grows in your life. You can encourage Godly growth in your life by choosing to abide in Jesus, or you can encourage demonic growth by letting the powers of darkness plant seeds in your heart.

Abiding in Jesus includes trusting God to know what fruit needs to be developed in our lives. We patiently wait for God to bring the growth while we position our lives for optimal fruit. But, we also have to learn to surrender our idea of good fruit. We might think that we know the kind of fruit that God needs to grow in our life, but God knows better. God controls the fruit, but you also control certain decisions that align you with God's ideal growth plan.

Level 3: Process |
Chapter 11: Divine Pruning

Remember how I said that God knows what areas need to be developed in our life? This also means that God knows what methods will produce the kind of growth we need.

He is not just in charge of the outcome of our faithfulness. He is also in charge of the process. God knows what method will produce optimal growth in our individual lives. I'll say it another way. God doesn't just know our destination, He also knows how to best get us there.

God knows what training program we need to go through to experience more good fruit in our lives, and God's training program involves suffering and persecution. This doesn't mean God is the author of these things, or that these things are good. This just means that as the devil brings suffering and pain into our lives, God sovereignly uses the enemy's schemes and attacks to strengthen believers.

This is exactly what Joseph says to his evil brothers in Genesis 50:20.

Genesis 50:20 - As for you, **you meant evil against me, but God meant it for good**, *to bring it about that many people should be kept alive, as they are today.*

Joseph responds to all the evil his brothers had committed against him. He was going to be murdered by them but instead they sold him into slavery. Then they lied to their father about Joseph's supposed death. Joseph then, experienced much heartache and suffering as a result of being sold into slavery. His brothers were the cause of most of his suffering and pain.

Now, years have passed since they sold Joseph into slavery. They're terrified that he will deal harshly with them, and Joseph answers their fears. He says that what they meant for evil, God meant for good. He doesn't deny that they wanted to harm him, but he acknowledges an even greater reality, which is that God intended to bring blessing and good through their evil actions. God's sovereign good plan overrides their wicked actions.

Master Chess Player

God is the ultimate chess player. He's countered every attack of the enemy. God is the master of re-direction. As the enemy throws a punch at God's people, God has already sovereignly re-directed the enemy's fist at his own big dumb face. This is the power of our God.

So, we have to understand that God will not always spare us from suffering and persecution.

Chapter 11: Divine Pruning

Sometimes He will help us avoid those things, but often, God uses the battle to strengthen His people for their good. Without the challenge, we will not grow. So, we have to learn to see suffering and persecution as a natural part of this broken, sinful world, but also as part of our divine training program. This is the kind of idea that what we see in Romans 8.

> Romans 8:28 - *And we know that for those who love God **all things work together for good**, for those who are called according to his purpose.*

God orchestrates EVERYTHING (not just some things) in our life for the good of His children. The context of Romans 8 suggests that suffering is the primary thing that God is working out for our good. This includes pain, trials and persecution.

But, what is the "good" that God is working out through everything we face? What is God's definition of "good" here in this passage? Paul explains this in the next verse.

> Romans 8:29 - *For those whom he foreknew he also predestined **to be conformed to the image of his Son**, in order that he might be the firstborn among many brothers.*

According to Paul, God's people were chosen by God for the purpose of being conformed to the image of the divine Son, Jesus Christ. In other words, God's purpose for choosing us was that we might be transformed into the likeness and image of Jesus.

God's definition of "good" is this: that which makes us most like Jesus in our thoughts, words, attitudes and actions. Now, ask yourself this question. Is this your idea of ultimate good? Do you see your life circumstances through the lens of God's definition of "good?"

I had to ask myself these exact questions, once I understood the "good" God wants for us.

One day I was reading this passage, and the Holy Spirit convicted me big time. I was not pursuing God's idea of "good." I had foolishly assumed that when God works all things for my good, this means that He will do what makes me most safe, healthy, comfortable, and at ease. But, I was reading these ideas into the passage. God does work all things together for our good, but we have to submit to His definition of "good."

God is moving His church in the direction of the ultimate good, which is the glorification of their bodies and their complete sanctification into the image of King Jesus. Everything is working out towards THIS ultimate purpose which is the greatest good. God is changing us more into the image of Jesus through every situation we face, and eventually we will be resurrected to glorified bodies where we are perfectly transformed into the image of Jesus.

Every detail of human history comes together to move the church towards the end goal of uniting ALL things under the feet of King Jesus. This must be our ultimate idea of good as we evaluate our life. This isn't just about God working out personal good for the individual but ultimate good for the whole church.

God's definition of good is what makes us most ready to see Jesus. It's making us most prepared for Heaven. It is making us most like Christ as possible. It is the highest level of sanctification and holiness possible in this life for us. God is bringing us as close to perfect conformity to Christ as He's determined possible in this life.

This is His definition of good. Now I have to constantly evaluate my heart to make sure that I'm pursuing God's definition of good rather than my own. Everything will change once you begin seeing your life circumstances in light of God's idea of "good." God is strategically using everything in our lives to shape our hearts and character into the image of Jesus.

The Master Potter

God is the master potter. And, He has an assortment of tools that He uses to carve out the best possible lives for us. But, our best life on earth is less about circumstances and more about how close we are to Jesus. And often, God's tools include the enemy's schemes, which includes suffering, pain and persecution. God doesn't delight in our pain and suffering, but He does delight in benefitting us through the attacks of the enemy.

> *James 1:2-4 - Count it all joy, my brothers, when you meet trials of various kinds, 3* **for you know that the testing of your faith produces steadfastness**. *4 And let steadfastness have its full effect, that you may be perfect and complete, lacking in nothing.*

James makes it clear that God is working through the trials of this life, because He knows what needs to be developed in us. We can count it joy when we encounter unexpected trials, because we know for certain that God is at work perfecting and maturing us into the image of Jesus.

And, if we value spiritual growth, we'll celebrate the fact that God knows exactly what will produce the right outcome in our lives. We can trust Him to handle our trials for our good like the Master Potter that He is.

We often think of God's blessings as coming packaged in the most luxurious, beautiful packages. But, often God's blessings come packaged in trials and suffering. The maturity you're praying for might just come packaged in another battle. The growth and good fruit you've been hoping for might just come packaged in persecution or trials.

We shouldn't only receive God's blessings as long as they're packaged a way that we like, because things aren't always as they appear. God doesn't just use what we prefer. He even uses what we prefer to avoid. God's training program for you includes suffering and trials. You might want to write that down for later in your life.

Let me bring you back to John 15 so you can see this clearly.

> *John 15:1-2 - I am the true vine, and my Father is the vinedresser.* **2** *Every branch in me that does not bear fruit he takes away, and* **every branch that does bear fruit he prunes**, *that it may bear more fruit.*

This is how our relationship with God works. God the Father is the vinedresser, or the owner of the vineyard. Jesus is the vine that supports the branches. And, we are the branches that remain connected to Jesus. This relationship to God helps us make sense of why God treats fruitful branches the way that He does. I don't know if you saw this at first, but Jesus says that the Father takes away fruitless branches and prunes the fruitful branches.

Now, I understand why God would punish the fruitless branches, but why would God punish the fruitful branches? God isn't punishing the fruitful branches; He's pruning them. There's a difference. God prunes fruitful branches because He is pleased, not because He's angry. As the owner of the vineyard, God wants more good fruit from His vineyard. This is why God takes action to make branches more fruitful than they already are.

God knows there's a better life for us and He does what ever is necessary to move us towards that, because He is a good, loving Father.

The Reward For Fruitfulness

So, what is pruning? I'm not someone that claims to know anything about agriculture, but I do know that if you want to make a tree more fruitful, you have to cut away those areas that are dead, because they're obstructing fruitfulness. Pruning means cleansing, purging or removing anything dead or useless that is slowing down fruit production.

And, this is exactly what God does to His people. He removes what is slowing down or even preventing fruit production in our lives, so that we can experience a more fruitful life.

And, how does God accomplish this? God uses suffering, struggle, difficulty and trials that the enemy brings against us in order to remove what is killing good fruit in our lives. These dead areas can be anything from sinful behaviors and thoughts to unhelpful addictions.

So, pruning is a reward for faithfulness because it moves us into greater fruitfulness.

It's precisely because we're growing in our faith that life gets harder and pressure comes to bring us to a new level in our relationship with God. Without the difficulty and pruning, we won't grow.

There may be certain sins, relationships, habits, addictions, and coping mechanisms that God is stripping you from, in order to make you more fruitful. And, the way God does this is through suffering and trials that cause us to rely on Him rather than those dead things we've trusted in for so long.

Trials have a unique way of exposing just how unreliable the vain things in our life are. But, without the trials, we'd continue relying on these things instead of God, which would lead to a life of limited fruit.

Here's what we have to understand as we're being trained up by God: God can always help us bear even more good fruit. God doesn't want His people to stay at the level they're currently at, because He knows there's more for us. God doesn't just want fruit, He wants more fruit. This is what a Good Father does. If God knew there was a better life for us and He didn't move us towards that life, He wouldn't be a loving Father. He wants more for us.

Chapter 11: Divine Pruning

This doesn't mean that God isn't pleased or honored by our good fruit. But, this does mean that God is always moving us towards greater fruitfulness, because this glorifies Him and benefits us more. The more fruitful we are, the more enjoyable our life will be. God is moving us towards the greatest human experience on earth, by helping us to bear more good fruit.

And, how does God do this? He prunes back the fruitful branches. Practically, this means that God brings His faithful children through greater battles to make them more fruitful. Remember, God works all things together for the good of His children, and "good" means more like Jesus, which is good fruit.

Pruning might seem painful in the moment, but it is incredibly beneficial for us in the long run.

> *Hebrews 12:11 -* **Now no chastening seems to be joyful for the present, but painful**; *nevertheless, afterward it yields the peaceable fruit of righteousness to those who have been trained by it.*

The author of Hebrews reminds God's people that the discipline and training of God isn't always enjoyable in the moment. In fact, it is often painful to be put through the fire. But, we are promised that God is training us towards greater faith and perfecting us into the image of Jesus. The discipline of God is not punishment for sin, but reward for faithfulness.

Of course, there are natural consequences for sin that God allows us to experience as a natural result. And, God does train us through those consequences. But, the discipline being described here, is the pruning or training that God puts us through to make us more like His Son, which is good.

But, do we see pruning as beneficial to our lives? Most often, we don't. Hopefully this will help you rightly frame up the pruning in your life, because the right frame will result in the right response. We want to respond faithfully and honor God by receiving the work He wants to accomplish in our hearts through the trials of this life.

God is increasing our capacity through heartache and pressure. Without trials, we wouldn't be able to manage the more that God has for us. Our capacity is directly related to our maturity.

In other words, the more that we are like Christ, the more we can handle and manage for the glory of God. God transforms His people through His own divine methods, and one of His methods is using suffering and persecution in this life for our good.

But, there is another way that God trains His people up into the image of Jesus which is what we'll explore in the next chapter.

Level 3: Process |
Chapter 12: Temptation Exposed

When it comes to our faith training program, God uses all of the enemy's schemes and turns them against the enemy for our good. One of God's divine training methods is using the enemy's attacks against us. This means trials and suffering, but it goes even beyond this.

The enemy does more than just make our life difficult.

In order to understand the enemy's schemes better, we have to read Jesus' words in John 10. I want to expose the devil's plan for you. The kingdom of darkness has a strategy and God exposes it for us so we can make the appropriate preparations.

> John 10:10 - **The thief does not come except to steal, and to kill, and to destroy**. *I have come that they may have life, and that they may have it more abundantly.*

The goal of the enemy is to steal, kill and destroy. This is the agenda of the kingdom of darkness. Every single scheme and strategy of satan and his demons, is designed to steal God's glory and lead people into spiritual death and eternal destruction.

We've already established that the enemy leads people to sin in order to separate them from God. This is spiritual death. God has decreed that the just consequence for sin is eternal separation from His presence. Psalms 5:4 tells us that sin cannot dwell in the presence of God, God. This is why the enemy leads us into evil. Sin disrupts our fellowship with God.

But, the powers of darkness are very strategic in the way that they accomplish this dark agenda. And, PRAISE GOD that the devil's plan is exposed in Scripture in order to give us the upper hand.

As hard as it is to believe, there is a method to the madness. The kingdom of darkness aims to separate us from God through sin, but the devil has a very strategic way of leading us into sin. It is called temptation. And, this temptation is actually apart of God's training program for us.

That sounds insane at first, but hear me out. I'm not saying that God temps us to sin. That would be a violation of both God's word and His character. James 1:13 says this very clearly.

> James 1:13 - Let no one say when he is tempted, "I am being tempted by God," for **God cannot be tempted with evil, and he himself tempts no one**.

So, God cannot be temped and He cannot tempt anyone to sin. But, what does it mean that God uses temptation as part of His training program for His people?

> Matthew 18:7 - "Woe to the world for temptations to sin! For **it is necessary that temptations come**, but woe to the one by whom the temptation comes!

Chapter 12: Temptation Exposed

In this passage, Jesus actually says that temptation is necessary, in the sense that it is unavoidable. We live in a world where temptation is just apart of the broken system. Of course, we can avoid certain temptations by using Godly wisdom, but temptation cannot be entirely avoided in this life. It is apart of this broken, sinful world, and especially apart of our sinful flesh.

But, God is faithful to use the temptation of the enemy in order to bring His name glory.

God Uses Temptation?

How in the world could a perfectly holy God use temptation for the good of His people? Check this out. Every single time you're tempted to sin, you're faced with two options. You can either honor God or rebel against Him in your thoughts, words, actions or attitudes. When I choose to honor God and obey His word in the midst of another option, God is glorified through my obedience and decision to love Him.

Not only that, but God trains and matures us through each victory He brings us into. Every spiritual battle that God helps us win is glory to His name. So, again, God is not the one tempting us. But, God has sovereignly allowed the devil and his demons to bring temptation against us. Though the devil intends to break us down, God intends to build us up. Though, the powers of darkness intend to dishonor God's name, God intends to glorify His name.

These battles with temptation are actually necessary in order for us to truly choose God and glorify Him. We can only love and obey God in this life when there is another option to rebel against Him. So, God intends to give us victory over temptation and bring us through the battle, and He does this by providing a way of escape every time.

> *1 Corinthians 10:13 - No temptation has overtaken you that is not common to man. God is faithful, and he will not let you be tempted beyond your ability, but* **with the temptation he will also provide the way of escape, that you may be able to endure it**.

God doesn't provide the temptation, but He does provide the strength to get through it. We have to understand that our God sovereignly allows spiritual battles to take place in our lives because He's strengthening us and bringing glory to His name. When we stand strong by God's Spirit and take the way of escape that God provides, God's name is made great.

But, I really want you to understand the nature of temptation. Many Christians are quick to blame demons for all temptation, but James tells us that sometimes our temptation comes from our own flesh without the intervention of demons. Our own sinful nature is capable of tempting us without any outside influence. Our sinful flesh desires sinful things. Period.

> *James 1:14 - But each one is tempted when he is drawn away by* **his own desires and enticed**.

Part of the enemy's strategy was to infuse our human body with the inherent desire for sin. This is the result of the fall. We want what is sinful and contrary to God without any help from the powers of darkness. Of course, there are times where temptation is amplified by the forces of darkness, and we're in the midst of heated, spiritual warfare.

Chapter 12: Temptation Exposed

There are even times where demons will capitalize on the sinful desires our flesh already has. But, sometimes our fleshly body just craves sin. We have a tendency to tempt ourselves.

The Serpent's Perspective

And, there are three primary categories for every temptation you'll face in this life. The Apostle John exposes all three kinds in 1 John 2:15-16.

> 1 John 2:15-16 - Do not love the world or the things in the world. If anyone loves the world, the love of the Father is not in him. For **all that is in the world—the lust of the flesh, the lust of the eyes, and the pride of life—is not of the Father but is of the world**.

Did you notice the three categories of sin? In this passage, we see the lust of the flesh, the lust of the eyes, and the pride of life. All three of these categories cover every kind of temptation humanity will ever face. Let's break this down.

The lust of the flesh is what feels good to the body. The lust of the eyes is what looks good to the eyes. And, the pride of life is what seems good to the human heart. Every temptation you'll ever encounter will either be based in what feels good, looks good, or seems good.

Once I understood how to recognize temptation for what it was, I began to experience much more victory over temptation. I learned to recognize what specific category of sin I was dealing with, which really helped me address that temptation the right way.

But, the devil wants to keep us in the dark about his schemes so we don't recognize the kind of temptation we're dealing with. When you misdiagnose the temptation, you'll be more likely to make the wrong decision about how to fight back.

Just know that whenever we're fighting temptation, we're fighting the desire to do what feels good, looks good, or seems good to our deceitful heart. Now you have categories for every temptation the enemy will ever bring against you. I'm telling you, when you understand the devil's strategy, you'll experience way more victory over sin.

Remember, temptation is just another part of God's training program for His people. Though, God doesn't want His people to sin, and He'd rather not have temptation at all, He sovereignly works with the broken, world system we're apart of.

Our God is so strong and wise, He incorporates every one of the enemy's schemes into our faith-growing program. If our God wasn't unstoppable, then He'd avoid those things He couldn't use for our good.

But, there is absolutely nothing God can't use for our good. This is why God doesn't always lead us around the valley. Instead He often leads us right through it, because He's such a capable Shepherd.

> *Psalm 23:4 -* **Even though I walk through the valley of the shadow of death**, *I will fear no evil, for you are with me; your rod and your staff, they comfort me.*

David writes that he walks through the valley of the shadow of death, even though he's following the Lord, who is the good shepherd. Just because we're following Jesus faithfully, doesn't mean we'll avoid temptation entirely. There are definitely some temptations in our life that result from our own foolish decisions, and God wants us to avoid those. But, there are many temptations God has strategically designed to bring us through, for His name's sake.

I want to take you to Genesis 3 now, where we'll see these three categories of sin play out. It's one thing for me to tell you how sin works, and it's another thing for me to show you through the narrative of Scripture. Let's see this play out in Genesis 3.

In Genesis 3, Adam and Eve are in the Garden of Eden enjoying the goodness of God and His creation. One day, Eve is approached by a being referred to as "the serpent." There's a chance that Adam is there as well, just watching everything unfold, but that is a discussion for another day.

We know for sure that the serpent approaches Eve to deceive her into eating from the tree that God commanded her and Adam not to eat from. And, eventually Eve does give into the temptation of the serpent and she rebels against her God and Creator.

But, before Eve sinned against God, there was a process that took place. This process is so important for us to understand yet somehow many Christians don't know about it.

How did the serpent deceive Eve into sinning against The Lord? He deceived Eve by bringing her through the process of temptation. Temptation isn't just a moment; it is a process.

To understand this process of temptation, we have to look at what happened right before Eve decided to eat the forbidden fruit.

> Genesis 3:6 - *So when the woman saw that the tree was **good for food, that it was pleasant to the eyes, and a tree desirable to make one wise**, she took of its fruit and ate.*

In Genesis 3:6, the author describes how Eve sees the forbidden fruit. There is a descriptive way that Eve views the forbidden fruit right before she commits to rebellion. And, what's interesting, is that Eve views the fruit according to the three categories of sin in 1 John 2.

Did you notice the three categories of sin in this verse?

Eve saw the forbidden fruit as something that was good for food, which is the lust of the flesh. The forbidden fruit was something that would feel good to consume. It would be satisfying to her physical appetites. Have you ever had a temptation that would feel good to your body?

Then, we see that Eve saw the fruit as something pleasant to the eyes. It was really attractive and enjoyable to look at. This fruit appeared good to Eve, which is the lust of the eyes. Has there ever been a time where you just gave into temptation because it looked attractive?

The last description of the fruit is that Eve saw the fruit as something desirable to make one wise. This means that Eve viewed the forbidden fruit as something that would make her know good and evil like God did. This would allow her to be

Chapter 12: Temptation Exposed

her own "god" because now she could define good and evil on her own terms.

No longer would she rely on God to define good and evil for her. She wanted autonomy and the forbidden fruit was her golden ticket. This is the pride of life of we saw in 1 John 2. Have you ever wanted something that would eliminate your need for God, or even allow you to stand in the place of God?

The sad thing is that Eve didn't get what she was promised. She didn't know good and evil like God did. Instead, she knew good and evil in a different way. She experienced evil for herself by rebelling against God. She knew evil through personal participation. This is not how God knows evil.

She wanted to have God's wisdom and knowledge without God in the equation. This meant that she would enjoy life outside of God's authority. But, that was not an enjoyable experience. Eve did not get what she thought she would through sin.

This is the nature of temptation. It always overpromises and under-delivers. And, temptation will always fall under one of these three main categories. Before Eve ever sinned, she saw the forbidden fruit from the serpent's perspective. In other words, she saw temptation from the tempter's point of view. This is what always happens before someone commits sin.

The Serpent's Conversation

The tempter wants you to go after what feels good, looks good or seems good. The devil wants us to follow our unguided heart that isn't submitted to God, because our heart is naturally inclined towards evil without the intervention of God's Spirit.

Jeremiah 17:9 - "The heart is deceitful above all things."

Our heart is deceitful. We need God to guide our hearts, but the devil wants to guide our hearts instead. The serpent wants us to adopt his evil, rebellious perspective of sin so that we adopt his ways. When we adopt the devil's perspective, we naturally adopt his ways.

But, before Eve saw the forbidden fruit from the serpent's perspective, there was a certain conversation she had with the serpent. This conversation influenced her perspective. See, the enemy wants to have a certain kind of conversation with us, because this conversation plants his thoughts into our hearts so that we're more likely to have his perspective.

If Eve avoided this conversation entirely, she might have never given into temptation. We're more likely to give into sin when we entertain the voice of the serpent like Eve did. But, if we can be aware of the kind of conversation that leads to sin, we'll be way more equipped to stand strong in the heat of temptation. Let's expose this deceptive conversation.

The enemy has one primary purpose behind the conversations he has with people. He wants to attack the truth of God in order to present a deceptive image of sin. If every temptation involves a conversation with the enemy, then every time we give into sin, we are believing a false idea about God and His word. The enemy attacks the truth of God. Period.

Chapter 12: Temptation Exposed

Whether or not we give into temptation, depends on what we believe about God and His word. The enemy strategically minimizes our view of God's word, so that we're more likely to rebel against God. This is the goal of every conversation the enemy has.

But, even within this conversation, the enemy has three primary ways of attacking truth. The powers of darkness will not always attack the word of God the same way, but we can at least be aware of how God's word will come under attack so we can prepare accordingly.

God's training program for us not only includes temptation but it even prepares us to faithfully endure temptation. God wants His people prepared for the spiritual battle, and He prepares us very well in His word.

Remember, in Genesis 3, the serpent wants Eve to adopt his perspective of God, and this takes place through a deceptive conversation that attacks God's word. Through that conversation, Eve chooses to see God how the serpent presented Him, rather than according to what she actually knew of God. And, by believing a false idea about God, she inevitably believes a false idea about the forbidden fruit.

Let's continue reading in Genesis 3 to develop a clear idea of how the enemy attacks truth.

> *Genesis 3:1-5 - Now the serpent was more crafty than any of the wild animals the Lord God had made. He said to the woman,* **"Did God really say**, *'You must not eat from* **any tree in the garden**'*?" The woman said to the serpent, "We may eat fruit from the trees*

in the garden, but God did say, 'You must not eat fruit from the tree that is in the middle of the garden, and you must not touch it, or you will die.'" **"You will not certainly die," the serpent said to the woman. "For God knows that when you eat from it your eyes will be opened, and you will be like God, knowing good and evil."**

This is the conversation that takes place before Eve sees the forbidden fruit differently. In this conversation, the serpent creeps up to Eve and spares no time tempting her. He gets right to the point, by opening with, "Did God really say?"

This one subtle question is packed with meaning. The serpent is subtly doubting God's command not to eat the forbidden fruit. The serpent is pretty much mocking what God had commanded by presenting God's command as something that sounds absurd and unbelievable. Not only is the serpent doubting the authority of God's word, but he's also doubting the goodness of God's character.

The serpent wants Eve to believe the lie that God has no intention of benefitting her. In the serpent's mind, God isn't looking out for Eve. God doesn't want Eve's ultimate good. We know this is a massive lie, yet this is the subtle lie that we're tempted to believe every single day when we're faced with temptation.

We're tempted to believe that God's commands aren't actually what's best for us. Instead of following God, we're tempted to follow our heart because we think we know better.

Chapter 12: Temptation Exposed

So, the first way the serpent attacks God's word is by doubting His word. If the enemy can get us to doubt the goodness of God or the benefits of His word, we will be more vulnerable to temptation.

The second way the serpent attacks God's word is by distorting what God commanded. I don't know if you noticed this, but the serpent misrepresents what God originally commanded.

God commanded Eve not to eat from ONE specific tree, but the serpent suggests that God isn't allowing Eve to eat from ANY tree in the garden.

Do you see the difference? One perspective makes God very generous, and the other perspective makes God very restrictive and selfish.

In the midst of temptation, the serpent wants us to see God as restrictive and selfish for keeping us from what we want, whether it be what looks good, feels good or seems good.

The good thing is that Eve defends God and corrects the serpent, but then she misrepresents God's command by adding another command He never gave. Eve says that they are allowed to eat from every tree in the garden, except one. She states that they aren't allowed to eat from the tree of the knowledge of good and evil, or even touch it, but God never said that.

God never told them that they couldn't touch the forbidden fruit. Eve added that extra command in her own mind. As soon as she finished her statement, I'm sure the serpent said, "Yup, I got her now." He knew at that point that she had distorted God's word in her own mind. She might not have distorted it as badly as the serpent did, but she still had a corrupted view of God's command in her mind. This is where things go downhill.

Why is it such a big deal that Eve adds another layer to God's command? Here's why. In Eve's mind, God's law is a burden that keeps her from enjoying life, and now God is some killjoy who wants to keep her from having fun. But, 1 John 5:3 says the opposite about God's law.

> *1 John 5:3 - For this is the love of God, that we keep his commandments. And **his commandments are not burdensome**.*

God's commands are not burdensome; they are life-giving. But, in Eve's mind, God's command was extremely unreasonable, and He was being unfair. This is what increased the likelihood of Eve giving into temptation. In her mind, disobedience would be justified because God had unrealistic expectations in the first place, right? Since God is being SO unreasonable, Eve has an excuse for disobeying such a restrictive command.

I don't know about you, but as a kid, I disobeyed my parents a lot. In fact, that disobedience escalated into my late teenage years. But, many times I did whatever I could to excuse my disobedience in my own mind.

One of my tactics was to make my parents out to be super unreasonable. If they were telling me to do something that was unfair, then there was nothing wrong with my

Chapter 12: Temptation Exposed

disobedience. If they were being unreasonable, then my rebellion was excused, right?

At least this is what I thought, but, now that I'm older, I realize that I wasn't excused to disobey them like I wanted to believe.

I just had a wrong view of my parents and their rules, which made me take the wrong action. In other words, I was rebelling against a wrong idea of who my parents were and what they wanted. I wasn't disobeying who they actually were or what they actually wanted for me. I was disobeying a fabricated version of my parents and their rules. Can you relate to this?

This is exactly what's happening in Genesis 3 with Eve. She makes God out to be some hard, unreasonable lawgiver that doesn't want what's best for her or Adam. In fact, in Eve's mind, God wants to ruin her fun and restrict her life. God is holding her back. At this point, she has officially adopted the serpent's view of God and His rules.

Now Eve is more likely to sin because she has a distorted view of God and His word. But, when she does sin, she won't be sinning against an accurate view of God. She will be rebelling against a false image of God and a faulty understanding of His command.

Eve is officially vulnerable to the final attack of the serpent. The last thing the serpent does is blatantly deny God's word and authority. After doubting and distorting God's word, the serpent outright denies God's word.

How is the serpent able to convince Eve that God is a liar, when this seems like such an obvious attack on God? How did Eve fall for such an elementary strategy? After falling for the first two subtle lies, Eve is now positioned to believe this outright lie about God. The serpent can blatantly deny God's word in a way that Eve will gladly entertain and receive, because she entertained the voice of the serpent too long.

Eve has already said that God promised death if they ate the forbidden fruit. She knows the consequences, but the serpent outright tells Eve that God is lying. The serpent says that Eve won't surely die, but instead, her eyes will open so that she will be like God. She will know good and evil like God. This is the serpent's final blow.

This conversation with the serpent is what made Eve susceptible to temptation. Now, as she looks at the forbidden fruit, she sees it differently. She sees sin through the eye of the enemy.

Have you ever viewed sin differently than God says in His word? This usually happens because we entertained the voice of the enemy too long. We should walk away from the conversation, but we listen to his voice much longer than we should.

God's Battle Strategy

Let's recap. The enemy has a conversation with Eve where he doubts God's word, distorts it, and eventually denies God's word outright. By attacking truth, the serpent is grooming Eve to be vulnerable to temptation. Through his conversation, the

Chapter 12: Temptation Exposed

enemy is causing Eve to see from his perspective by planting seeds of deception in her heart.

The serpent wants Eve to have a different view of God, His word, and the forbidden fruit. Then, Eve sees the forbidden fruit through the eyes of the enemy. In Eve's mind, the forbidden fruit is no longer something bad for her. Now, it's something that looks good, seems good, and will feel good to eat.

And, BAM! Eve gives into temptation and eats the forbidden fruit which she then shares with her husband (who seems to be present the whole time?). This is how the enemy gets people to sin against God. Sadly, this includes believers who choose to sin against their own Father.

But, now that you understand the devil's strategy, you will be way more equipped to face temptation. You'll see way more victory over sin now that you understand how the enemy tempts you to sin. If we can learn how to cut off these mental conversations with temptation, we'll be one more step ahead of the enemy.

Remember, the enemy wants you to entertain mental conversations with him. He wants you to entertain his voice long enough that you eventually give into temptation. But, here's what I suggest. End the conversation. I know this sounds easier said than done, but have you ever just hung up the phone on a telemarketer?

I get these telemarketing calls all the time, and one of my favorite things to do is to answer the phone only to end the call after a long, drawn-out silence. Once I answer the phone,

I say absolutely nothing. I just let the telemarketer sit there in silence. Then, once they speak up, I immediately end the call just to mess with them.

They usually don't call back anymore because it's such a pain to deal with me. But, this is how we should deal with the enemy. We need to have the discipline to end the call. I know what you're probably thinking. "How in the world do we cut off a mental conversation? We can't just run away from our thoughts, can we?"

You don't have to run away from your thoughts. God has given you the power to take evil thoughts captive as your prisoner. You have the God-given, spiritual ability to throw evil, tempting thoughts into a mental prison where they can't influence you.

> 2 Corinthians 10:5 - We **destroy arguments and every lofty opinion** raised against the knowledge of God, and **take every thought captive** to obey Christ,

Paul tells us that we can take thoughts captive in submission to Jesus and His word.

Let me practically show you what this looks like in Matthew 4, where Jesus stares darkness in the face and doesn't even flinch.

In Matthew 4, Jesus is led into the wilderness by the Spirit of God where He will be personally tempted by the devil. The embodiment of darkness is coming to personally attack the Son of God. This is a showdown for the ages, but it is definitely not a competition.

Chapter 12: Temptation Exposed

Even after fasting for forty days and nights, Jesus is unstoppable. The devil tempts Jesus three separate times with the exact same three temptations we saw in 1 John 2 and Genesis 3.

Jesus is tempted with what looks good, feels good, and seems good. The enemy has the exact same battle plan to get Jesus to sin. But, unlike Adam and Eve, Jesus resists temptation perfectly and remains completely obedient to the Father. He doesn't sin even once.

I want to show you how Jesus remains victorious over sin. I don't just want to expose the devil's strategy against you, but I also want to provide God's battle plan for you.

Just to be clear, we are not on the defensive. God's people are on the attack. This is what Jesus says in Matthew 16:18 to Simon Peter.

> Matthew 16:18 - And I tell you, you are Peter, and on this rock I will build **my church, and the gates of hell shall not prevail against it**.

Jesus says the gates of hell cannot stand against His church. This means the powers of darkness are locked up in a city and those gates cannot keep out God's people. There is no defense system that can keep God's children from plundering the kingdom of darkness.

So, just like Jesus in Matthew 4, we are not the weak victims hiding behind the city walls from the devil and his demons. It is quite the opposite.

In Matthew 4 it may seem like Jesus is a victim, but He is indeed the victor. Let me show you exactly how Jesus fights back against the devil in all three temptations. Jesus models what it looks like to faithfully stand strong against sin.

Each time, Jesus verbally answers back with Scripture. Look at it.

> Matthew 4:4 - But **he answered,** "**It is written**, "'Man shall not live by bread alone, but by every word that comes from the mouth of God.'"
>
> Matthew 4:7 - **Jesus said to him,** "**Again it is written**, 'You shall not put the Lord your God to the test.'"
>
> Matthew 4:1-10 - **Then Jesus said to him**, "**Be gone, Satan! For it is written**, "'You shall worship the Lord your God and him only shall you serve.'"

In every temptation, notice that Jesus quotes the Old Testament. This is how He fights the devil's temptations. Jesus stands on the word of God and conquers sin every time. But, what I find interesting is that Jesus doesn't just remind Himself what God's word says.

He doesn't just mentally rehearse Scripture. He audibly quotes the Scriptures, and wields God's word like the master swordsman He is. And, the devil can't stand under the power of God's word.

Jesus' weapon of choice is the sword of the Spirit, which is the divinely authoritative, unchanging, infallible word of God. Jesus doesn't just know Scripture, He uses it. He doesn't just

Chapter 12: Temptation Exposed

embody Scripture as God, He submits to Scripture as man. And, what we have to understand is that our spiritual battles are going to be no different.

God has given us one weapon, which is His word, but, it's our choice whether or not we'll actually swing our sword in the heat of temptation. Once I paid close attention to how Jesus uses Scripture, everything changed for me. He uses His voice to proclaim God's word. I wish I knew this growing up in the midst of overwhelming temptation.

I wish someone told me that knowing God's word wasn't enough, but I had to choose to submit to that word, rely on it, and audibly recite it.

Now, this might be the first time you're hearing this, and it might sound superstitious, but notice how Jesus isn't fighting back until He unleashes the word of God from His mouth.

Temptation is destroyed when the word of God is unleashed. We are not fighting back until we're actually quoting Scripture. This might sound unrealistic at first.

What if you're in public? What if it's nighttime and everyone is asleep? God's methods for your victory don't change. God has ordained that His word is your weapon, but He will not force you to wield it. Whether you whisper scripture or scream it at the top of your lungs, verbalize God's word somehow and trust God to deliver you from temptation.

The next time you're tempted, you need to have a list of Scriptures on hand and ready to go. I recommend that these verses speak to the specific temptation you're dealing with.

You might have to write these down on a notepad and hang it above your bed. You may have to make these verses the lock screen on your phone or the background on your computer. You might even have to tape these verses on your bathroom mirror. Whatever you have to do in order to have these Scripture accessible in your heart and visible to your eyes, do it.

There are times where I'm in the middle of temptation and I don't even think about quoting God's word. I just forget. Sometimes I don't even consciously recognize the fact that I am in the middle of spiritual warfare. I might have Scriptures memorized word for word but if I don't remember those verses in the midst of temptation, what good is it for me?

This is why I've found it helpful to have my "battle Scriptures" accessible and visible where I'm often most tempted. That's right. You and I both know there are certain physical locations where temptation is heightened for you. You know that if you sit in that room, get around those people, or lay in that bed, temptation increases exponentially.

But, when I have my "battle Scriptures" as accessible as possible where I can visibly see them, I'll remember to fight with God's word. If I see the word of God with my physical eyeballs, I'm reminded to stand on His word and wield the word of the Spirit.

God's divine training program involves temptation, but if we're not prepared for spiritual battle, we'll be defeated by the very thing that God intended to strengthen us with.

Level 3: Process |
Chapter 13: The Fruitful Life

God has the best possible life available for you. The most abundant and satisfying life is a fruitful life, and God promises that you will be fruitful if you choose to abide in Him. When you choose to abide in Jesus every day, there will be a certain kind of life you will experience.

You will be a fruitful person that lives an abundantly, blessed life, and this is what God wants for you. Jeremiah 17:7-8 tells us what a fruitful life practically looks like for us.

> *Jeremiah 17:7-8 - "Blessed is the man who trusts in the Lord, whose trust is the Lord. He is like a tree **planted by water**, that sends out its **roots by the stream**, and **does not fear** when heat comes, for its **leaves remain green**, and **is not anxious** in the year of drought, for it **does not cease to bear fruit**."*

Jeremiah tells us that whoever trusts in the Lord will be blessed. This abundant, fruitful life is described in three different ways.

Planted By Water

First, Jeremiah says this fruitful person is like a tree that is planted by water, and sends out its roots by the stream. This means they are planted, secured and well-supplied. A tree that's planted by water is well-nourished, and its roots go deep which make it secure. So, this tree is planted well, which means it isn't easily shaken. This tree is stable and won't be uprooted easily.

The fruitful life is one of security and provision because that person is planted. What does it mean that a believer is planted? Jeremiah 17 tells us that these planted individuals have chosen to trust in the Lord which is why they're like a tree planted by abundant water.

Christians are those who trust in the Lord for righteousness, salvation, and eternal life, and by doing so, they plant themselves in the Lord. Psalm 92 also brings clarity to this.

> Psalm 92:13-14 - **They are planted in the house of the Lord**; they flourish in the courts of our God. They still bear fruit in old age; they are ever full of sap and green,

This idea of being planted has to do with proximity to God. The Psalmist says that the righteous person is planted in the house of the Lord, which simply means that they dwell in the presence of God. This isn't a moment of being in the presence of God, but a lifetime of dwelling near Him.

If you want to be fruitful for God, you have to be close to God. There's a profound connection between fruitfulness and our closeness to God. Intimacy with our Father is key to fruitfulness.

Those who trust in the Lord will experience a lifetime of security in Christ. This means that the storms of this life won't easily shake them or move them. They are stable because their soul is anchored to the Living God. This provides stability and consistency to the fruitful Christian. This is part of our heritage as believers.

We might not always live secure, but this consistent security and stability is available to us in Christ as we choose to abide in Him.

See, God draws us near to Him to make us fruitful for Him. The presence of God brings stability to our life. Our fellowship with God brings security to our soul that nothing can touch.

Constant Fruit. No Fear

There is a second description in Jeremiah 17. Jeremiah says that the fruitful, righteous person is not anxious or afraid of the heat or drought, which represent the trials of life.

God's best life for us includes freedom from fear of the future, fear of uncertainty, and fear of trials. Some of the biggest fears in my life have revolved around the uncertainty of my future and the trials in this life. But, as I've grown closer to Jesus, I've seen tremendous growth in these areas.

The closer I am to God, the less afraid I am of the future, because the more I trust Him.

Jeremiah tells us why the fruitful person isn't afraid or anxious. They aren't afraid because their leaves remain green and they don't cease to bear fruit. This is the third description of the fruitful believer. Psalm 92 says that the believer flourishes, which is another way of saying, nothing can stop Christians from bearing fruit.

The attacks of the enemy cannot stop us from bearing fruit. The trials and sufferings of this life cannot prevent us from producing good fruit. Not even temptation can kill our fruitfulness. In fact, God uses these things to produce more fruit in our lives. These attacks can actually make us more fruitful if we continue to abide in Jesus.

God has wired us to be fruitful in spite of our life circumstances rather than because of them. In other words, we aren't fruitful because of how good our life situations are. We are fruitful because of how good our God is. God has filled us with His Spirit so that we are planted in His presence 24/7. And, our proximity to God is what makes us fruitful.

This is why the fruitful, righteous person isn't afraid. They know for a fact that in every season and environment, they will be bearing good fruit because of their unstoppable God. Fruitful Christians are confident even in the face of difficulty, struggle, hardships and suffering. They know that Jesus is enough and nothing can stop God from bearing good fruit in their lives.

There's something so powerful about realizing that our good fruit is not dependent upon our life circumstances. We can be in any environment, whether it be drought, flood, famine, or fire, and we will still be fruitful because we are in Christ.

Chapter 13: The Fruitful Life

God's people can't be stopped by the season of nature or the environment they find themselves in. We are planted and rooted deep in Jesus, who supplies us everything we need to be fruitful, regardless of the situation.

Again, we can flourish at any moment because of our closeness to God. We don't just get by. We don't have just enough to squeeze out one tiny fruit. God makes us flourish in any given situation, and this is because of His presence in our life.

This means we can be abundantly fruitful anywhere, anytime, in any situation. This is our confidence, and this is what we can be certain of. God said it, so we trust Him. We don't need to look to our life circumstances to figure out if we can be fruitful or not.

Fruitfulness depends on Jesus, not our environment.

> *Psalm 1:1-4 - Blessed is the man Who walks not in the counsel of the ungodly, Nor stands in the path of sinners, Nor sits in the seat of the scornful; But his delight is in the law of the Lord, And in His law he meditates day and night. He shall be like* **a tree Planted by the rivers of water, That brings forth its fruit in its season, Whose leaf also shall not wither; And whatever he does shall prosper.** *The ungodly are not so, But are like the chaff which the wind drives away.*

In this passage, David adds to the description of the fruitful, righteous person. In verses 3-4, David repeats what Jeremiah 17 and Psalm 92 showed us. He says that they are like a tree planted by rivers of living water, which allows them to bring forth fruit and never wither away.

Then, David adds that whatever they do shall prosper. This is the same idea of fruitfulness, but it refers to the work of their hands. This means that their efforts and labor will succeed even in the midst of opposing forces.

As Christians, our efforts are not in vain. Our labor has eternal value. Our work for God will matter in eternity, because God is making our labor fruitful. This is our confidence as we face the ever-changing seasons of life.

Sometimes we just need to remember that as believers, our life is not a waste as we continue abiding in Jesus. Our lives are accomplishing something that impacts God's Kingdom forever, because Godly success is part of the fruitful life.

Fruitful Decisions

I want to show you a couple of key ideas in the first two verses of this passage. David says that the blessed man doesn't walk in the counsel of the ungodly, stand in the path of sinners or sit in the seat of the scornful.

This is a progression. If we walk a certain way for long enough, eventually we'll stand there and get so comfortable that we sit there and plant our lives there. And David is saying that the blessed man will not walk in ungodly counsel, live in ungodly ways, or plant himself in a lifestyle of wickedness.

In summary, the fruitful person doesn't copy the lifestyle of unbelievers. They don't surround themselves with ungodly

Chapter 13: The Fruitful Life

people on a consistent basis. Their community is not composed of godless people that hate God.

This doesn't mean they don't evangelize and love the lost. This just means they aren't walking the same direction as ungodly people. They aren't joining unbelievers in their sin in the name of "evangelism" or in the name of "building relationships."

Fruitful believers don't receive counsel from people who don't have the mind of Christ. They don't do life with people who aren't going the same direction as them. In other words, they surround themselves with Godly community as they engage the lost world with the gospel.

We aren't called to neglect or avoid the lost people around us, but we also are told not to have our inner circle composed of pagan unbelievers. The fruitful Christian is someone who has chosen their community wisely. They surround themselves with people who will encourage growth in their life. Our core friendships are incredibly important for fruitfulness.

The last description of the fruitful person is that they consistently meditate on the word of the Lord. Not only is their mind focused on God's word, but their hearts delight in God's word. We meditate on what we value and love most.

Your thought life reveals your greatest affections. And, the fruitful person experiences an abundant life because of what they choose to meditate on throughout their day.

Meditation doesn't refer to mindless, vain repetition of God's word. Meditation refers to thoughtfully considering the word of God, and critically thinking through a passage over and over to develop better understanding about it.

This means we're choosing to intentionally think about God's word and how it applies to our life. We might even be considering how a passage reveals God and how it connects to other parts of Scripture. As God's word governs our mind, we'll see good fruit produced in our life.

But, meditation involves our heart as well. We don't just tolerate God's ways, we delight in His ways. God's word is something we genuinely enjoy and value because of how it reveals our Father to us.

Again, most of our thoughts revolve around what we love and value most. This is why the Psalmist says the righteous man meditates on God's word day and night.

As we're falling asleep, we should be dwelling on God and His word. While we're living our normal day-to-day life, we should be intentionally re-centering our thoughts around God's word. As we're waking up, we should be conscious of how God is giving us breath for another day, and this involves rehearsing what His word says about Him. This is a discipline, but it leads to the most fruitful life possible. I promise, I've seen this happen in my own life.

God's Blueprint For You

So, we know what a fruitful person will be like inwardly. But, the last thing we need to understand is what a fruitful person will do outwardly.

Chapter 13: The Fruitful Life

Everyone has their own idea about what kind of activity will accompany a fruitful life, but the only thing we care about is what God says.

We've already established that God desires good fruit. This is the main thing that God desires for His people. But, when God says He wants good fruit, He simply means that He desires for you to move towards Jesus while you move other people towards Jesus.

Everything we've discussed up to this point is about moving towards Jesus while moving others towards Jesus. This means we're becoming more like Jesus while helping others to become more like Him. Another way to say it is that we are becoming a better disciple while making other disciples.

All of these are different ways of communicating God's original purpose for humanity.

Remember, God commissions Adam and Eve to be fruitful and multiply. God always intended for humans to be His representatives in the earth, while they make more human beings who would image God in the earth.

God desires fruitfulness and multiplication. He doesn't want His work in us to stop with us. He wants it to flow through us into the lives of others.

This is why Jesus gives His disciples the great commission in Matthew 28.

> *Matthew 28:18-20 - And Jesus came and said to them, "All authority in heaven and on earth has been given*

to me. Go therefore and **make disciples** of all nations, **baptizing** them in the **name** of the Father and of the Son and of the Holy Spirit, **teaching them to observe** all that I have commanded you. And behold, I am with you always, to the end of the age."

Jesus calls His disciples to go and make disciples, and then He describes what that process looks like. His disciples are supposed to go and preach the gospel, then they're called to baptize those who believe in the name of the triune God. But, the work doesn't stop there.

Jesus also tells them to teach them everything He has taught them. This is what it means to make disciples. We don't make converts and then leave them on their own.

Making disciples involves walking with those who have trusted in Jesus for salvation. We are called to share what Christ has taught us in order to train them up in faith. Fruitfulness involves preaching the gospel and training up disciples in the word of God.

This is what it means to image God faithfully and bear good fruit. It means that we're growing into His image, reflecting His image and multiplying His image. This is what an abundant, fruitful life will look like. A fruitful person is continually growing up in Christ, representing God well, and making more disciples.

These are the three main things a fruitful person will be doing, but it goes even deeper. I want to be as helpful as possible and give you a visual representation of a fruitful life. So, here is an image that I like to refer to as God's blueprint for your life.

Chapter 13: The Fruitful Life

This is how we break down what it means to grow into, reflect, and multiply the image of God. I've broken those three categories down into seven key things that every believer should be doing in order to experience the most fruitful life possible.

This is what it means to move towards Jesus while moving other people His direction. When a Christian is doing all seven of these things, they will be walking in the fullness of God's purpose for them.

The danger is that we would treat this more like a checklist rather than a road map. A checklist is something we can mindlessly check off every day without being mentally present and enjoying what we're doing. A road map is something we constantly refer back to in order to make sure we're still going the right direction. This is how I want you to see this.

Don't let this guide become something that constantly discourages you because of all the things you're not doing, or all the areas you're failing in. I've been tempted to do that, and when I do, it only leaves me crippled rather than empowered to keep moving forward.

Let's break this down. The fruitful life involves growing into the image of Christ. And, the way we practically do this is by learning, gathering, and seeking. Let me unpack this idea of learning in the three different ways it happens best in your life.

Growing In Christ's Image

The first way to learn is through mentorship. Learning involves getting mentored by older Christians and learning from their experience and wisdom. Paul writes about mentorship in His letters, as Timothy was his spiritual son.

> 2 Timothy 2:2 - And **what you have heard from me** in the presence of many witnesses entrust to faithful men who will be able to teach others also.

Paul tells Timothy to teach others what he has personally learned and heard from Paul. Timothy's spiritual mentor was Paul, who had personally taken Timothy under his wing. Not only did Paul teach Timothy truth, but he even brought Timothy on his missionary journeys where Timothy learned from experience with Paul. This is biblical mentorship.

We need to have people in our lives who are spiritually farther along than us. Everyone needs a Paul and a Timothy in their life. They need someone to learn from and someone to teach. But, mentorship is not about lectures and the classroom. Mentorship also includes personal experience where two people are sharing their lives and following Jesus

Chapter 13: The Fruitful Life

together. Iron should sharpen iron, which means that both mentor and student are teaching each other.

This doesn't mean you should only have one person in your life that you're learning from and being mentored by. It is actually wise to have multiple mentors who have different perspectives, journeys and levels of maturity. Maybe even have a different mentor for each area of your life. Don't limit yourself to just one mentor, but also don't be a student of anyone and everyone. Be very selective and prayerful about who you let speak into your life.

I'll be honest, this is one of the most neglected areas of my life. I've had several temporary mentors, but I have never had one main mentor for any large portion of my life. And, maybe this isn't completely wrong, but I can definitely work on developing more intentional mentorship relationships.

As you're intentionally seeking out Godly mentors, it is helpful to know that God will often bring different mentors in our lives for different seasons and reasons. In each season, we need something different, and each mentor can be God's temporary assistance for the season He knows we need that specific help.

It won't always be one main person you learn from your entire life. That may happen for some, but I believe God often brings multiple mentors into our lives at different times.

The second aspect of learning is gathering with other believers in order to grow and learn with them. Spiritual growth might be personal but it isn't isolated. God is growing us personally but it is never in a way that is completely disconnected from

His local church. Often, what God does in us will be for the benefit of other believers.

We have to learn how to view our spiritual growth alongside the growth of other believers in our lives. What God accomplishes in us will compliment what He's doing in the lives of those believers around us.

Growth won't just happen behind closed doors. It also happens in the context of a local community. God knows how to grow us best which is why He places us in a community with others believers who challenge us to grow.

God places His people in local church communities where they can gather together in order to encourage, comfort, challenge, convict and sharpen one another. God knows that we will often learn something only within the context of community. This is why God's method of growing you will often be through people that He surrounds you with.

Hebrews emphasizes the importance of gathering with other believers.

> *Hebrews 10:24-25 -* **And let us consider how to stir up one another** *to love and good works,* **Not neglecting to meet together***, as is the habit of some, but* **encouraging one another***, and all the more as you see the Day drawing near.*

Many Pastors will use these verses to command their congregation not to miss Sunday service, but this passage just speaks of the importance of gathering as believers. This is not just about one specific day of the week.

Chapter 13: The Fruitful Life

God desires for His people to be together, and it is most beneficial for us to be apart of a local church where we share our lives with other believers throughout the week. This can be at a coffee shop. This can be at your house. This can be at a small group outing at the park.

God just tells His people not to neglect each other.

We can become so self-centered and focused on our own spiritual growth that we neglect the people God has called us to serve, love, and benefit. Not only does spiritual growth happen best alongside other believers as we stay in community, but God works in our lives to benefit others.

One of the main reasons that God grows His people is so that they would improve the lives of others. Our spiritual growth directly relates to how helpful and beneficial we will be to those around us. Your faith is your own, but it is not just for you.

If you are growing closer to God, but you are disconnected from God's people, then no one benefits from your life. What is the point of God growing and developing you? If we are only concerned with spiritual growth because of personal gain, we don't understand spiritual growth how God does. The method and goal of our spiritual growth includes other believers.

If you read the book of Acts, you'll notice the church was praying together on a constant basis. Acts 1:14, 1:24, 2:1, 2:42, 3:1, 4:31, and 12:12 all emphasize the gathering of believers to pray and seek the Lord together. Why was the early church experiencing such explosive growth? I believe part of it was because of how seriously they took fellowship and prayer.

They gathered together with one heart to seek the presence and will of God, and this became their power to reach the lost world with the gospel. Unbelievers were being added to their number daily because of the tremendous love the church was displaying. They genuinely loved one another and gathered often. And, this exponentially multiplied their growth.

> *Proverbs 27:17 - Iron sharpens iron, and* **one man sharpens another**.

Just as iron can sharpen other iron, so God has deigned His people to sharpen one another. God will use my life to sharpen your faith. He will also use your life to sharpen my faith.

But, if we aren't sharpening other believers, improving their lives, or benefitting their faith, are we really following Jesus well? If you're not connected to a consistent community of like-minded believers, you have to wonder if you're growing as fast as you could be.

I've noticed in my own life that I've experienced accelerated periods of spiritual growth when I am consistently getting around other believers with one heart and one mind. I've also noticed that many times in my life, my spiritual growth was lacking because I had become too busy for God's church. I pulled away from God's people because my personal responsibilities were too much to balance with church. And, this is exactly what the devil wants for us.

Chapter 13: The Fruitful Life

The powers of darkness will make us too busy and stressed with our own personal lives. Then, we'll distance ourselves from the people that God uses to strengthen us and help us stay faithful. These are also the people God intends to benefit through our lives. We have to make sure we aren't becoming self-absorbed because this will often be to the neglect of God's people.

If we really want to experience tremendous fruit in our lives, we have to fight to stay in fellowship with God's people. God has decided to grow us more effectively into the image of Jesus when we are in consistent community with other Christians.

The third, and arguably most important way we grow into the image of Jesus, is through seeking God on our own. Our personal quiet time with God is more important than we know. And, this quiet time refers to seeking the Lord in prayer and in His word.

Now, this is where things can get tricky. We're supposed to seek God on our own as well as with other believers. But, I've seen many Christians over-emphasize either one of these to the neglect of the other.

For example, some people only have personal time with God in His word and prayer, and they never get around God's people. They're under the impression that their isolated, quiet time with God is all they need.

This is what I call the lone-wolf Christian. They're out fighting the devil and the powers of darkness on their own because they assume personal quiet time is all they need to effectively experience God's abundant life and calling for them.

On the other hand, you have believers that have zero quiet time with the Lord because their faith hangs on other believers in an unhealthy way. God wants us to realize that we need His church, but our church gatherings and small group bible studies CANNOT replace our personal quiet time with the Lord. We need both, and it is often difficult to balance these well.

I'm a person of extremes. I tend to swing towards one extreme and then over-correct to the other extreme. Sometimes I realize I haven't had much quiet time with the Lord and then, I'll cancel every meeting with other believers in order to seek the Lord alone.

From there, I'll usually realize that I haven't been around God's people in a while, so I'll make the necessary changes.

It is hard to have a healthy balance, but not impossible. God's purpose for our lives includes a healthy balance of personal quiet time and church gatherings, and the way that we seek the Lord personally is by having a set time every day to spend in prayer and God's word. We desperately need to have consistent time reading the Bible and praying.

We've already discussed the importance of God's word as it relates to our lives, but I want to briefly touch on prayer.

Many people think prayer is just something you do once a day for a set period of time, and I used to think this too. But, prayer is a lifestyle. Yes, we should have those set times where

Chapter 13: The Fruitful Life

we dedicate long periods of time to prayer, but that should overflow into the rest of our day. We should do our best to remain in constant communication with the Lord all day.

1 Thessalonians 5:16-18 - Rejoice always, 17 **pray without ceasing**, *18 give thanks in all circumstances; for this is the will of God in Christ Jesus for you.*

I don't believe this passage commands that every moment of our day we should be in constant communication with God. While I believe that is ideal, and should even be our goal, I don't believe it is realistic.

This passage emphasizes the persistence and consistency of prayer. We shouldn't lose heart when we pray. We should consistently talk to the Lord on a daily basis while we demonstrate a child-like persistence as we seek our Father.

I don't want to get too deep into the concept of prayer, because I intend to write a book on prayer in the future. But, for now, I want to give you a helpful definition of prayer. I remember learning this idea from John Piper years ago, but I added some personal touches to it.

Prayer is talking to God with intention and purpose, as His own child, according to His word.

This definition of prayer has radically changed the way that I approach my quiet times with the Lord. When it comes to faithfully praying and reading the Bible, I believe we often have a misunderstanding of what this means practically.

Many Christians think they only need to read the Bible once a day and have one set time for prayer. And, while we should have a main chunk of time set aside to prayer and Scripture, it shouldn't stop there.

Let's say that you spend 30 minutes in prayer and 45 minutes reading God's word. That main time with the Lord should overflow into the rest of your day so that you meditate on His word and talk to God throughout your day.

I typically like to have my quiet time with the Lord in the morning because that main time with God is what positions my heart to follow Him throughout the rest of my day. I read the word of God in the morning so I have something to think through and meditate on later.

It is the same with prayer. I spend a large time talking to God so that I'm more likely to stay in communication with Him later on.

I'm not saying this is the perfect model that everyone should follow. Your quiet time with the Lord will be different because it'll be unique to you. But, this is just how I've come to learn how to prioritize my time with God. Whatever you have to do, prioritize your time with the Lord above all else every single day. This really is the most important aspect of our faith: a personal, growing relationship with our God.

And, as you seek the Lord in prayer and Scripture, God will grow you in exponential ways that might not always be immediate or obvious. But, He is growing you. If we want to grow into the image of Jesus, we CANNOT neglect our personal quiet time with God.

But, this daily time with the Lord has to be accompanied by fellowship with other believers.

> 1 Chronicles 16:11 - **Seek the Lord** and his strength; **seek his presence** continually!

The nation of Israel is told to seek the Lord and His presence continually. For Israelites in the Old Covenant, this meant that they would go to the temple of God in Jerusalem to worship the Lord through praise, offerings, sacrifices, and times of dedicated prayer. This also involved hearing the reading of God's Law from the priests.

As believers in the New Covenant, this means something a bit different for us. For us to seek God's presence means that we're opening our Bible to be closer to the Lord and know Him deeper. It means we're spending time in prayer to experience His very near presence on a daily basis, because we need Him. Either way, seeking God assumes you intend to find him.

Seeking the Lord has to be your priority in life, because everything else will flow from this.

So, let's re-cap. In order to grow into the image of Christ, we have to be learning, gathering, and seeking.

This means we are:

1) Being discipled or mentored by someone who is farther along in their faith.
2) In consistent community with other like-minded believers.
3) Consistently seeking the Lord in prayer and His word.

Reflecting God's Image

As we are doing our part to grow into the image of Jesus, we will naturally begin to reflect the image of Jesus. Reflecting His image will happens in two primary ways.

Reflecting the image of Jesus means that we will be serving and obeying. Let's address the idea of spiritual service first.

The most practical way to serve God is by serving His people, and this assumes that we have something to contribute to our brothers and sisters in Christ. Every single believer has been gifted by the Holy Spirit with what we call spiritual gifts. God has gifted us in order to be a gift to His people.

So, whatever gifts you have, are not primarily for you, but for the benefit of others. God has given you unique, spiritual gifts to build His church and make other people's lives better.

> *1 Peter 4:10 - As each has received a gift,* **use it to serve one another***, as good stewards of God's varied grace:*

Peter tells the church that they should use their spiritual gifts to serve one another. This is what it means to faithfully manage the gracious gifts that God has given to them. So, there is a framework for how we should use our spiritual gifts.

We should use our spiritual gifts to promote unity in the church, benefit God's people, and glorify the name of Jesus.

God has gifted His people in such a way, that each of us has a gift that the rest of the church needs. When we use our spiritual gifts, we are being used by God to fill the gaps of what the church is missing.

Your local church community needs you to use your spiritual gifts and play your God-given role. This shouldn't boost your ego, but should emphasize how gracious God is for using you to supply His people.

When God's people aren't using their gifts, or are using their gifts for an inappropriate purpose, the church will suffer loss. We each have a unique role to play in the body of Christ, but that requires us to know our role, our gifts, and the purpose for these gifts.

When everyone is humbly serving with their gifts to benefit each other, God's people will be taken care of the way God desires.

The second aspect of reflecting the image of Jesus is obedience. Obeying God is crucial to the abundant Christian life. Jesus says this in John 14 to His disciples in the upper room.

> *John 14:15 - "If you love me, **you will keep my commandments**."*

Jesus is hours away from being arrested and crucified and He tells His disciples that they will keep His commandments if they truly love Him. But, Jesus explains that His commandments are simply to believe in His words and love one another.

In other words, Jesus desires for His disciples to believe in His message which will naturally produce love for each other.

*John 6:29 - Jesus answered them, "This is the work of God, that you **believe in him whom he has sent**."*

*John 15:12 - "This is my commandment, that you **love one another** as I have loved you."*

Growing obedience is a necessary requirement for the fruitful, Christian life. And, growing obedience starts with believing in the gospel message of Jesus. Once a person believes the gospel, they'll begin growing in love for people in order to love as Christ has loved them.

I use the word "growing" on purpose because I don't want Christians thinking that God demands perfect obedience for them to get into Heaven.

We are only getting into God's Kingdom because of our faith in Jesus, but growing obedience is a necessary sign of true saving faith in Christ. Our life will progressively conform to the image of Jesus, as we do everything to promote spiritual growth in our life.

So, reflecting Jesus faithfully means that our life is in obedience to His commands.

One of the greatest ways we can experience the presence of Jesus in our lives is by walking in His commands, and His commands outline perfect love. Every command of God will be about loving God or someone else. The ten commandments outline what perfect love will look like.

Whenever we violate one of God's commandments, we are inevitably choosing not to love God or someone made in the image of God. Reflecting the image of Jesus means that we are serving God's people and obeying God's commands. Then, as we do this, we will be fulfilling the law of love and giving the world an accurate picture of who God is.

> John 13:35 - By this all people will know that you are my disciples, **if you have love for one another**."

When we love each other through Godly service and obedience to God's word, the world will know that we truly are disciples of Jesus. Every Christian holds a small piece of the picture of Jesus. When we play our role, love one another, and use our gifts to serve one another, we are coming together to form the beautiful mosaic of our Savior Jesus.

Multiplying God's Image

The last thing we're called to do is multiply the image of Jesus. As we reflect the image of God well, we will naturally come across opportunities to multiply the image of Jesus by making disciples. This includes preaching and teaching.

Evangelism and discipleship will be part of a fruitful, Christian life.

We are called to preach the gospel of Jesus. How God calls us to do this will be unique to our personality, experience, and gifting. Every believer is called to preach the gospel in varying degrees. But, this is a part of the abundant Christian life. Trees don't bear fruit just for us to look at. That fruit is supposed to be enjoyed and consumed in a way that satisfies our hunger.

This is exactly why God produces good fruit through His people. We don't bear fruit just for show. Our fruit isn't just purposed to impress people and gather crowds. God produces good fruit in our lives so that others might eat from the tree of our life and enjoy the goodness of God. Our good fruit should point people to Jesus in order for their soul to be satisfied.

So, when we produce good fruit, we have to remember, that God intends for others to enjoy and consume the good fruit that our lives produce. Our good fruit should plant seeds in other people which will produce good fruit in their lives. This is what we call evangelism and discipleship. Our fruitful life should validate the message we preach.

Many people might think they aren't called to preach the gospel or make disciples because they don't "have these gifts" or it doesn't come naturally to them. But, Jesus commissions all of His disciples to share the good news of salvation with whomever God leads them to.

Of course, everyone will share the good news in varying degrees, but we are all called to preach to someone. Whether we water, plant or harvest, God has given each of us a sphere of influence. I can't reach the people in your life that only you have a unique connection to, and the same is true with you. We each have God-given relationships that we have been uniquely designed for.

> *Romans 10:14-15 - How then will they call on him in whom they have not believed? And how are they to believe in him of whom they have never heard?* **And how are they to hear without someone preaching?**

Chapter 13: The Fruitful Life

> *And how are they to preach unless they are sent? As it is written, "How beautiful are the feet of those who preach the good news!"*

In Romans 10, Paul emphasizes the importance of preachers being sent into the world. And, you might not call yourself a preacher, but everyone is called to share the good news on some level. These opportunities to share Christ should come naturally through your God-honoring life.

In other words, our fruitful life of obedience and service should create reasons for people to want to know the God we serve. God creates opportunities for us to evangelize as we just simply follow Him faithfully each day. Our faithfulness should naturally create opportunity to evangelize and give people reason to believe what we preach.

This doesn't mean we won't have a responsibility to act on these opportunities. We need to be aware of these opportunities and ready to give a defense of the hope we claim to have.

> *1 Peter 3:15 - but in your hearts honor Christ the Lord as holy,* **always being prepared to make a defense to anyone who asks you for a reason for the hope that is in you**; *yet do it with gentleness and respect,*

Peter tells the church to be prepared to defend the faith. This means that believers are actively engaged and training for these moments where God leads them to share the good news of Jesus. We need to seek the Lord in such a way where we are anticipating these opportunities to evangelize. In fact, growing in Jesus, assumes that God is preparing us for these unplanned moments where we will get to share Jesus.

But, God doesn't just call us to preach the gospel. He desires for us to train up those whom He saves. God desires for us to be a mentor in someone else's life. Everyone of us should have a Timothy in our life, where we are teaching and training them up in Jesus.

Remember, what God teaches us is not just for us. God intends for us to teach others what He has revealed to us. This is real faithfulness. Biblical faithfulness is not merely applying what we know but passing down what we know.

In Matthew 28, Jesus commissions His disciples to go and make more disciples who would follow in His ways. Making disciples involves preaching the gospel, but it doesn't stop there. If we only preached the gospel, and did nothing else, we would have an entire world of baby Christians who wouldn't be capable of living the Christian life.

> *1 Peter 2:2 - Like newborn infants, long for the pure spiritual milk, that by it you may **grow up into salvation**.*

A group of baby Christians won't make for a great church. Peter tells Christians to long for the spiritual milk of God's word in order to grow up into the things that are hard to understand. Babies can't have steak. They need milk because that's all they can handle. But, as they grow up, they can handle more mature food.

Believers aren't able to handle the deeper things of God's word when they're spiritual infants. They need to grow up in the basic teachings of Jesus, which involves more mature believers teaching them and leading them through these things.

God's people are called to mature in Christ, by growing up in the truth of God, and God grows new believers through the teaching of older believers. This means that discipleship has to happen in the church. Mature believers should take younger believers by the hand to lead them through what God has personally taught them. Discipleship is simply choosing to intentionally move someone else towards Jesus by teaching them what you have learned.

This doesn't mean that we only disciple people in the classroom with a whiteboard. In fact, discipleship probably won't happen best in this kind of setting. Discipleship happens when we choose to share our lives with younger believers. This means that most of our teaching will happen with our lives. Jesus lived with His 12 disciples for 3 and a half years. They pretty much went everywhere together with a few exceptions. They ate together and slept in the same place. They experienced almost everything that Jesus did.

Throughout those 3 and a half years, Jesus would stop frequently to intentionally teach them the truth of God's word. But, these moments of teaching were complimented by Jesus' life. His lifestyle is what reinforced His teachings to His disciples so that they saw truth demonstrated for them. This is how we should see discipleship.

Making disciples is absolutely essential to the Christian life. If God originally commissioned Adam and Eve to multiply through childbearing, and Jesus has primarily commissioned

His disciples to multiply disciples, I can confidently say that multiplication is the mark of a fruitful Christian life.

Fruit possesses seed that will naturally produce more fruit when that seed is planted in the ground to become a fruit-bearing tree. Within every kind of plant is the inherent ability to self-replicate, whether it be through seed, spores, or another method.

If trees didn't reproduce, our world wouldn't be what it is today. But, specifically within fruit trees, God has placed seed that will grow into other fruit-bearing trees. Multiplication is the mark of a fruitful, healthy tree, because the seed is inherently part of the fruit.

Discipleship is the mark of a fruitful, healthy believer who is living the abundant, Christian life. Abundance isn't just about benefitting self, but other people.

True abundance overflows into the lives of others.

What I'm trying to get you to understand is that good fruit will always be multiplied in the lives of others. If fruit tastes good, but doesn't plant seed in the ground for more fruit trees, that fruit just terminates on itself. This kind of fruit is enjoyable but it is only temporary.

Eternal Investment

Real, good fruit will extend beyond the life of the original tree. Even if a tree should die, the seed that comes from that tree will still grow up into other trees. And, those trees will

Chapter 13: The Fruitful Life

produce other trees even if the original tree is dead. This is just like what Jesus says in John 12.

> John 12:24 - Truly, truly, I say to you, unless a grain of wheat falls into the earth and dies, it remains alone; but **if it dies, it bears much fruit**.

In this context, Jesus is referring to His death and resurrection. His death would make way for the seed of His Spirit to take root in His disciples, which would activate their spiritual ability to bear good fruit as new creations in Christ.

As disciples of Jesus, our fruitfulness is only possible because Jesus died for us. He laid down His life as a kind of seed that would be planted in the ground to make way for more fruit trees like Him. We are those fruit trees that follow in His footsteps.

> John 16:7 - Nevertheless, I tell you the truth: it is to your advantage that I go away, for **if I do not go away, the Helper will not come to you**. But if I go, I will send him to you.

Jesus says that He needs to leave for His Spirit to fill His people permanently. We don't have the Spirit of God without Jesus' sacrificial death. We don't have the resurrection of Jesus without His body being buried.

The death of Jesus made way for us to be filled with His Spirit and re-created as new human beings in His image. Jesus made disciples by literally planting His life in the ground to produce more trees that would bear fruit just like He did.

The church is still going strong today because Jesus' sacrifice produced fruit that would outlast his temporary 33 years on earth. The fruit of His sacrifice (His church) is His legacy.

I don't know about you but I want good fruit that outlasts my life. I want to leave a legacy that matters. And, God says His church is what matters. I don't just want my life to bear good fruit that stops when I die. Our lives should bear generational fruit. Our lives should plant seed in the lives of others who will plant seeds in others.

Real abundance will outlast our temporary life. If your idea of good fruit only impacts you, then I have to let you know that you aren't thinking big enough. Jesus didn't just die for those alive in His day. His resurrection impacts all of human history.

1 Corinthians 15:20 - But now Christ has been raised from the dead, **the first fruits of those who are asleep**.

Jesus' resurrection becomes the first of resurrected humanity. We will follow in His footsteps one day because of His decision to lay down His life for others. We will be resurrected with Jesus because He made way for us to follow in His footsteps.

If we are truly making disciples, we are going to move people in the direction of that ultimate resurrection where we will be glorified with Jesus on the new earth. True discipleship is preparing people for eternity with God. This requires us to lay down our life so that we're thinking beyond our lives.

So, who are you training up in Christ? Is there anyone in your life that you can begin teaching and training up in God's word? You might not know everything but you know something. Especially, after reading this book, you know enough to be effective in this life. Practically, you can share this book with someone else and bring them through these essential truths.

Maybe you don't understand these truths in a deep enough way to effectively teach people. You might not be a teacher by nature, but, maybe you can lead a small group where you and a few others just read through this book together and talk about it. This is discipleship.

Take younger believers through a book of the Bible that you confidently understand and help them make sense of those incredible truths.

Meet one on one with one or two younger believers throughout the week. Maybe you can start a small group with a few newer believers that you know of. Whatever God is placing on your heart, God intends to produce fruit through your life.

And, the most abundant life will be experienced when we choose to start living for others. The fruitful, Christian life is about investing into others and training up effective disciples for Jesus. Discipleship is necessary if you truly want the fullest Christian life. This isn't about benefitting self, this is about being effective.

Do you really want to be effective in this life? When you see the King of Kings face to face, don't you want to know for sure that you pursued a fruitful life that honors His name?

*Ephesians 4:1 - I therefore, a prisoner for the Lord, urge you to **walk in a manner worthy of the calling** to which you have been called,*

Paul calls us to live a life that is worthy of the calling we have in Christ. We want to live worthy of the gospel and our King who saved us. If God has planted so much in us, then He expects a return on His investment. Our God desires good fruit that multiplies His image. There is a kind of life that most honors God and is best for you.

God desires for His people to be constantly growing, which means we are being mentored, we are gathering with other believers, and we're seeking the Lord daily.

He desires for His people to be constantly reflecting His image honorably, which means we are serving the church with our spiritual gifts and obeying the commandments of God to love.

And, lastly, God desires for His people to be multiplying His image in the earth, which requires us to share the gospel message and train up younger believers in the ways of Jesus.

The kind of life that is worthy of Jesus, is a life that is growing into the image of Christ, reflecting His image, and multiplying His image of the earth. This is the blueprint for the most fruitful, Christian life possible. This is our purpose until God calls us home. In every decision, in everything you can possibly do, keep moving people towards King Jesus.

Printed in the USA
CPSIA information can be obtained
at www.ICGtesting.com
LVHW042004120923
757612LV00002B/232